SEP - 2021

W9-BGK-658

WITHDRAWN
Woodridge Public Library

W. JORDSEN PUBLIC LIBRARY
MILL HOSE II CA?-5014
(800) 204-7008

CULTURES OF THE WORLD
Mali

WOODRIDGE PUBLIC LIBRARY
3 PLAZA DRIVE
WOODRIDGE, IL 60517-5014
(630) 964-7899

Cavendish
Square

New York

Published in 2022 by Cavendish Square Publishing, LLC
243 5th Avenue, Suite 136, New York, NY 10016
Copyright © 2022 by Cavendish Square Publishing, LLC

Third Edition

No part of this publication may be reproduced, stored in a retrieval system, or transmitted in any form or by any means—electronic, mechanical, photocopying, recording, or otherwise—without the prior permission of the copyright owner. Request for permission should be addressed to Permissions, Cavendish Square Publishing, 243 5th Avenue, Suite 136, New York, NY 10016. Tel (877) 980-4450; fax (877) 980-4454.

Website: cavendishsq.com

This publication represents the opinions and views of the author based on his or her personal experience, knowledge, and research. The information in this book serves as a general guide only. The author and publisher have used their best efforts in preparing this book and disclaim liability rising directly or indirectly from the use and application of this book.

All websites were available and accurate when this book was sent to press.

Library of Congress Cataloging-in-Publication Data

Names: Blauer, Ettagale, author. | Lauré, Jason, author. | Denton,
  Michelle, author.
Title: Mali / Ettagale Blauer, Jason Lauré, and Michelle Denton.
Other titles: Cultures of the world (third edition)
Description: Third edition. | New York : Cavendish Square Publishing, 2022.
  | Series: Cultures of the world | Includes bibliographical references
  and index.
Identifiers: LCCN 2021012732 | ISBN 9781502662712 (library binding) | ISBN
  9781502662729 (ebook)
Subjects: LCSH: Mali--Juvenile literature.
Classification: LCC DT551.22 .B58 2022 | DDC 966.23--dc23
LC record available at https://lccn.loc.gov/2021012732

Writers: Ettagale Blauer, Jason Lauré; Michelle Denton, third edition
Editor, third edition: Michelle Denton
Designer, third edition: Jessica Nevins

PICTURE CREDITS
The photographs in this book are used with the permission of: Cover Peter Adams/Stone/Getty Images; p. 1 Geraint Rowland Photography/Moment/Getty Images; p. 3 Atlantide Phototravel/Corbis Documentary/Getty Images; pp. 5, 48, 60, 62, 68, 74, 76, 78, 88, 96, 103, 114, 115 Wolfgang Kaehler/LightRocket via Getty Images; pp. 6, 46, 79 commerceandculturestock/Moment/Getty Images; p. 7 Claudiovidri/Shutterstock.com; p. 9 STRINGER/AFP via Getty Images; pp. 10, 51, 81 DeAgostini/Getty Images; p. 13 Sascha Grabow/Moment/Getty Images; pp. 14, 17, 121 Remi Benali/The Image Bank/Getty Images Plus; pp. 15, 20, 126 john images/Moment/Getty Images; p. 16 Matt Fletcher/Lonely Planet Images/Getty Images Plus; pp. 21, 56, 69, 86, 90, 122 MICHELE CATTANI/ AFP via Getty Images; pp. 22, 98, 100 Olivier Martel Savoie/The Image Bank/Getty Images Plus; p. 24 Harry Hook/The Image Bank/Getty Images Plus; p. 27 DEA/A. DAGLI ORTI/De Agostini Picture Library/Getty Images; p. 29 Janet Kimber/The Image Bank/Getty Images Plus; p. 31 Michel HUET/Gamma-Rapho via Getty Images; p. 32 Keystone-France/Gamma-Keystone via Getty Images; p. 35 JEAN HOUNTONGBE/AFP via Getty Images; p. 36 ANNIE RISEMBERG/AFP via Getty Images; pp. 38, 44 mtcurado/iStock/Getty Images Plus; p. 41 Photo 12/Universal Images Group via Getty Images; p. 42 Xinhua/via Getty Images; p. 49 Lily FRANEY/Gamma-Rapho via Getty Images; pp. 53, 64, 93 nik wheeler/The Image Bank Unreleased/Getty Images; p. 58 Alf/Moment/ Getty Images; p. 63 Ondrej Prosicky/iStock/Getty Images Plus; p. 66 Hugh Sitton/Stone/Getty Images; p. 70 Alain PETIT/Gamma-Rapho via Getty Images; p. 71 Kimberley Coole/Lonely Planet Images/Getty Images Plus; p. 83 Riccardo Lennart Niels Mayer/iStock/Getty Images Plus; p. 87 SOULEYMANE AG ANARA/AFP via Getty Images; p. 94 CommerceandCultureAgency/The Image Bank/Getty Images Plus; pp. 105, 112 Icodacci/iStock Unreleased/Getty Images; p. 108 H. Christoph/ullstein bild via Getty Images; p. 109 Owen Franken/Stockbyte/Getty Images; p. 118 Maremagnum/The Image Bank Unreleased/Getty Images; p. 124 Bruno Barbier/robertharding/Photographer's Choice/Getty Images Plus; p. 129 Friedrich Schmidt/Photographer's Choice/Getty Images Plus; p. 130 Paul_Brighton/Shutterstock.com; p. 131 AS Food studio/Shutterstock.com.

Some of the images in this book illustrate individuals who are models. The depictions do not imply actual situations or events.

CPSIA compliance information: Batch #CS22CSQ: For further information contact Cavendish Square Publishing LLC, New York, New York, at 1-877-980-4450.

Printed in the United States of America

Find us on

CONTENTS

MALI TODAY

MALI IS A VAST NATION—THE EIGHTH LARGEST IN AFRICA. IN Bambara, Mali's most widely spoken language, its name means "hippo," though Mali does not have much wildlife. It is often called the crossroads of Africa because great civilizations and empires were born there. Caravans have traveled across Mali on trackless sands, navigating by the stars, guided by centuries of experience. It is a place where history comes alive around every turn in the road. Despite recent turmoil, Mali remains true to its vibrant cultural heritage and celebrates the many ethnic groups that make up its population. In a country where friendly greetings are of the utmost importance, it is hard not to feel welcomed by the people of Mali.

SWEPT AWAY BY THE DESERT

Much of Mali is part of the Sahara, a desert that covers most of North Africa. Desertification is pushing the population southward as the Sahara creeps into once-fertile lands. With little rainfall and sand slowly replacing plant life, growing crops and

Women and girls do most of the farming in Mali.

keeping livestock are becoming increasingly difficult. These staples of everyday life still support survival even in the country's harshest regions, but Mali remains poor because there is little left over to sell to international markets.

Despite these hardships, life in Mali goes on. People farm, raise large families, play soccer, and drink a lot of sweetened green tea, all on the edge of the desert. This is due, in part, to Mali's position along the banks of the Niger River, which brings water to an otherwise dry country.

A LAND OF MANY CULTURES

Mali is very diverse. With nine major ethnic groups and many other small ones represented, there are lots of cultures constantly mixing throughout the country. As the largest ethnic group in the country, the Bambara people have

influenced Mali's culture and language more than any other group. Mali also is home to two fascinating and complex cultures, the Tuareg and the Dogon. Their different ways of life help define the nation of Mali. In many ways, they spell out the history of the region and show how people adapt to extremely difficult climates and geography. They have also survived many periods of foreign rule, including European colonization.

Even though there have been recent cases of ethnic violence between the Dogon and the Fulani, the second largest group in Mali, most Malians get along with their neighbors regardless of their differences. They are united by a common history and the religion of Islam, and cultural traditions are often shared among groups living close to each other. Yearly festivals invite the whole country to celebrate and enjoy the music, dances, and crafts of Mali's many varied cultures.

The Dogon live on top of a remote plateau. Although some Dogon people have integrated into mainstream Malian society, their culture remains separate.

THE THREAT OF RELIGIOUS EXTREMISTS

Over the past decade, radical Islamic groups have taken over many cities in northern Mali. The kind of militant and strict Islam being promoted by these groups is far from the Islam practiced by most Malians. Muslims are generally people of peace, but fringe extremists believe violence is the only way to enforce Islamic law. These people are commonly known as jihadists, and they use terrorist tactics such as bombings and kidnappings to try to achieve their goals.

It is believed that Islamist (Islamic extremist) terrorist groups saw the barely populated region of northern Mali as a good place to recruit people to their cause. Unfortunately, there are many young men there with little or no education and no chance of employment who can be won over with money and a promise that they are fighting for a worthwhile cause. The upheaval in this region has created instability across the country as refugees from invaded towns flee south and terrorist attacks increase in frequency.

Although Mali is receiving help from other countries to combat the jihadist infiltration, the government has done relatively little to protect its citizens. Because of this, as well as for other reasons, the military staged a coup d'état and took control of the government in 2020.

UNDER MILITARY RULE

Mali has been taken over by its military four times since it gained its independence in 1960. In 1968, 1991, and 2012, political and economic issues boiled over into mutiny and saw each president at the time removed from office by force. Social scientists believe this pattern began because Mali's army was not established until after colonial rule had ended, making the military a protector of the people rather than a tool of European oppression. Therefore, the Malian army feels it is their duty to defend the country at all costs, even against its own government.

The 2020 coup was no exception. In August, the military stormed the capital city and held President Ibrahim Boubacar Keïta and other government officials

hostage until they resigned and dissolved the government entirely. A military-majority interim government has since been formed, but the international backlash has put Mali in a precarious position. With invaluable aid being choked off, the citizens of Mali can only hope that the new government will treat and defend them better than the old one.

People in the capital city of Bamako celebrated the 2020 coup as the armed forces paraded into Independence Square.

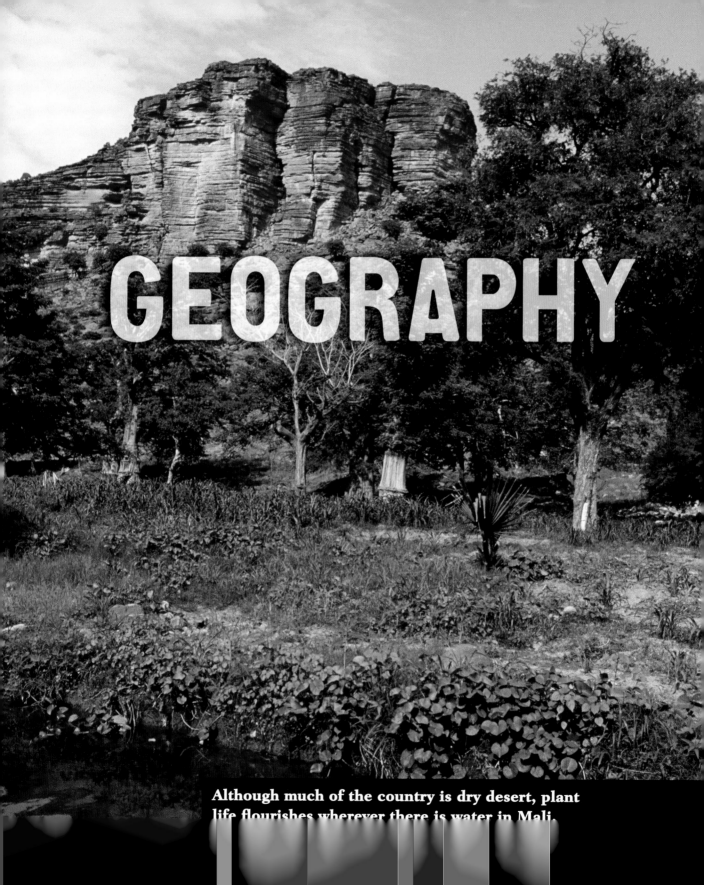

GEOGRAPHY

Although much of the country is dry desert, plant life flourishes wherever there is water in Mali.

1

MALI IS A LANDLOCKED COUNTRY that sprawls across northwestern Africa, covering 478,800 square miles (1.2 million square kilometers). Mali is about the size of Texas and California combined. The country is shaped somewhat like a butterfly tilted to one side. It measures around 782 miles (1,258 km) from the northwest to the southeast and 1,151 miles (1,852 km) from the easternmost border to the westernmost border. The entire northern half of the country lies within the vast Sahara. The Sahara makes life and travel extremely difficult for those living in that part of Mali. The only permanent settlements there are villages clustered around deep water sources called oases.

South of the Sahara is a shifting region of semidesert. This area is called the Sahel, from the Arabic word meaning "shore." The people who live there see the Sahara as a vast ocean of sand, while the shore is an

Mali shares borders with seven countries: Algeria to the north; Niger to the east; Burkina Faso, Côte d'Ivoire (Ivory Coast), and Guinea to the south; and Senegal and Mauritania to the west. Most of these countries were formerly part of French West Africa, and the divisions between them were drawn by the French according to their own bureaucratic needs. This is why the borders between Mali and Algeria and between Mali and Mauritania are so straight.

area that can support life. In the Sahel, it is possible to find grazing areas for livestock, which most Malians need to sustain life.

In Mali, geography determines how and where people live. When water holes dry up, the people who live in the Sahel move to the south. Some people try to find other areas to graze their livestock, but many are forced to move into towns even farther south. Those who live near the mighty Niger River use its water to irrigate their crops, water livestock, and keep households running. In general, the climate is growing drier, and more and more people are being forced to leave their traditional lands. The rapidly growing population forces people to grow crops in poor soil. This overuse of delicate land leads to further drying of the soil.

THE DESERT

The Sahara is a vast ocean of sand that covers almost all of North Africa. It measures about 800 to 1,200 miles (1,300 to 1,900 km) from north to south and about 3,000 miles (4,800 km) from east to west. It is mainly composed of hard-packed sand and mountains, with rock plains and the occasional oasis. Huge sand dunes are found in isolated areas.

The Sahara has not always been a vast desert. An inland sea once covered the land. When it dried up, the area became a fertile plain. Rock paintings found in the central Sahara show that people and wildlife lived there, with plenty of grazing land and vegetation. There were many wild animals, including giraffes, elephants, and antelopes, as well as herds of cattle. The people living there at the time had a comfortable life, with grassy plains supporting their livestock. Ten thousand years ago this region was green with vegetation. There was a shift in Earth's axis at that time that brought about an increase in both sunshine and rainfall, allowing wild grains to flourish.

About 7,000 years ago, the people living in the region began to form permanent settlements. They domesticated sheep to use for food and clothing. The rains that fell were absorbed by the earth and created underground reservoirs of water. This is the water that now feeds wells and oases spotted throughout the Sahara.

SANDSTORMS

When harsh wind blows across the Sahara, it picks up tiny particles of sand and whips them into a sandstorm. This wind, called the harmattan, carries fine, dry sand. It can bring the visibility down to zero and stop people in their tracks. The sky can be clear one moment and then totally obscured the next. The wind-driven sand gets into every tiny crack and crevice. A person who is outside must try to find shelter.

Sandstorms can block out the sun. To someone inside the storm, it becomes dark as night.

Over the next several thousand years, the climate changed again. Another shift brought less sun and less rain to the area. This region became the desert we now know as the Sahara.

The Sahara is a growing desert, constantly claiming more land. As the population grows and there are more people with herds of livestock, more grazing land is needed. People have moved their goats and other animals onto land that was once considered marginal, or land that can barely support any vegetation at all. Once the livestock eat all the vegetation, there is nothing to

Sand dunes are
constantly shifting,
making life in the
Sahara difficult
and unpredictable.

hold the moisture in the ground. The land becomes drier and soon gets covered with the sands of the Sahara. North of the town of Ségou, where the desert meets land with some vegetation, one can actually see this shift taking place.

It is not only flat land that is being taken over by the Sahara. About 15 percent of the Sahara consists of dunes. As the wind blows steadily out of the northeast, it pushes the sand up one side of a dune and down the other. It is a slow process, but over time, one can actually see a dune on the move. Travelers who have been coming to the region for 30 or 40 years remember when there were towns that had trees and other vegetation around them that are now completely deserted because the Sahara has moved in.

THE SAHEL REGION

The shift from Sahara to Sahel is an ongoing process. There is no real border between these two regions. The Sahel can support some crops, but this is dependent on the seasonal rains. In good seasons, when the rains come, farmers

can grow food. In poor seasons, when the rains fail, the farmers in this region are unable to grow enough food to sustain their families. In most of the Saharan region of Africa, the Sahel is shrinking, making it more difficult for people to find enough food for their livestock. This process is known as desertification. As more and more of the land dries up and becomes part of the Sahara, there is even greater pressure put on the remaining land. In some areas, the change is so abrupt that the line that divides the Sahara from the Sahel can actually be seen. In one section, the land has a small covering of green, and right next to it, it is covered in a film of fine sand.

The Sahel supports some plant life, but it is rapidly being taken over by the desert.

Further to the south, the savanna region of the country generally has the best climate. This is where most of Mali's people live.

FLATLANDS AND MOUNTAINS

Most of the land that Mali occupies is extremely flat. About 90 percent of the land consists of plains and plateaus. This flatness plays a very important role

The Tambaoura Escarpment rises high above the town of Kéniéba in western Mali.

in the way rainfall affects the land. By far the most important feature of the center of the country is the Niger River floodplain. It dominates the landscape as well as the life of the nation.

However, there are some notable exceptions. East of the Niger Valley, the Dogon Plateau is a highland area bordered by the Bandiagara Escarpment. These steep cliffs separate the Dogon people's land from the rest of Mali and have allowed the Dogon to maintain their own culture even though they are located in the geographic center of the country.

The cliffs of Bandiagara run 124 miles (200 km) to the Grandamia Massif, a mountain chain rising 3,543 feet (1,080 meters) in the eastern-central part of the country. Mount Hombori, the highest point in the country at 3,789 feet (1,155 m) tall, is found there.

In the hilly region of the southwest, where Mali borders on Guinea, are the Kéniéba Mountains. These mountains rise to heights of 1,312 to 1,969 feet (400 to 600 m).

The Bambouk Mountains, in the extreme western part of the country, run up against the Tambaoura Escarpment. This is next to Mali's border with Senegal.

Up in the extreme northeastern corner of the country is a sandstone plateau called the Adrar des Ifoghas. This is the southern end of the Hoggar Mountain Range that dominates southern Algeria.

Mali's lowest elevation is found at the Senegal River, just 75 feet (23 m) above sea level.

THE RIVER OF RIVERS

The Niger River flows across Mali from west to east and supports a major part of the nation's economy and transportation. The river starts to the west, in neighboring Guinea, and flows northeast toward the Sahara. About two-thirds of the way across Mali, it makes a great turn and heads south toward the border with Niger. This turn is known as the Niger Bend.

When the rains are plentiful and the Niger River is full, it helps support life. The river itself and the land on either side of it support many of the food crops grown in Mali.

The word "Niger" is believed to come from a Berber phrase, *gher-n-gher*, which means "River of Rivers." It is the third longest river in Africa, after the

The Niger River supports many communities on its banks and is responsible for most of Mali's agriculture.

There are several museums in Bamako, Mali's capital, each with a different way of presenting information about the country and its people. The Musée National (National Museum) shows Mali's history through art, artifacts, and exhibits of Malian textiles and also shows films about the history and cultures of Mali. The Musée du District de Bamako (Bamako District Museum) opened in December 2003 and also shows some of Mali's history, particularly during the colonial era, but it concentrates more on Bamako itself. The Muso Kunda, or Musée de le Femme (Woman's Museum), focuses on the role of women in Mali. It is a good place to see regional costumes and to sample African food in the museum's restaurant.

Nile and Congo Rivers. It runs for a total of 2,600 miles (4,200 km) through West Africa, and 1,050 miles (1,700 km) of that total is found in Mali. Its flow varies according to the time of year and depends on how heavy the seasonal rains are. During the rainy season, which varies throughout the country, 800 miles (1,300 km) of the river can be navigated. This allows people and goods to travel by boat from town to town. Virtually all of Mali's important towns are found along the path of the Niger River. Seventy-five percent of all the people in Mali live in the region that is crossed by the Niger River.

Although Mali has lost most of its wildlife, it still has desert-dwelling elephants and manatees that live along and in the Niger River.

INNER NIGER DELTA

In the last months of the rainy season, the amount of water in the Niger River increases until it begins to flood its banks and spread out into streams and lagoons. As the water level increases, it covers a vast area of the flat land. This floodplain is known as the Inner or Inland Niger Delta. It covers an area measuring 7,722 square miles (20,000 sq km). In the south, the rainy season usually runs from April to October. In the north, the rainy season may last only from July through September. The farther north, the less rain there is, even during the rainy season.

Whether the rains are heavy or light, the water that flows along the Niger River is greatly reduced during its journey through Mali. It is estimated that almost two-thirds of the flow disappears as it makes its journey between Ségou and Timbuktu, a distance of 372 miles (600 km). This happens because the water seeps into the sandy soil and also because of evaporation as it nears the Sahara. Water is also diverted by the Niger Basin Authority for irrigation.

The marshland, with its flow of fresh water, is used to grow rice, millet, and sorghum. Even in the area that is not flooded, the farmers benefit. They carry water to their fields in animal skins.

THE SENEGAL RIVER

Mali's other important river is the Senegal River, which begins its journey in southwestern Mali. It is formed by two rivers, the Bafing and Bakoye, which meet at the town of Bafoulabé in the westernmost part of Mali. This river flows to the northwest. Its main tributary is the Falémé River, which forms the Senegal-Mali border. The total length of the Senegal River is 1,020 miles (1,641 km). During the rainy season, boats can travel along the river as far as Kayes in western Mali. Kayes has a reputation for being the hottest place in all of Africa. On an average day, the high temperature reaches 95 degrees Fahrenheit (35 degrees Celsius), but in April and May, the average temperature is 104°F (40°C). The Senegal River also creates a floodplain that is much smaller than that of the Niger River. Rice is grown within the floodplain. River water is also used to irrigate other crops.

CLIMATE AND RAINFALL

Mali has two seasons—wet and dry. April to October is generally the wet, rainy season, while November to March is the dry season. These seasons vary in different regions of the country, naturally, with the Sahara being hotter and much drier than the savanna to the south.

Mali is one of the hottest countries in the world. Average temperatures year round are between 80°F and 85°F (27°C and 29°C). In April and May, temperatures reach 95°F to 104°F (35°C to 40°C). The hottest period is from

March to July, when temperatures often exceed 100°F (38°C). In the Sahara, daytime temperatures often rise above 110°F (43°C). At night, temperatures in the winter months in the Sahara can plunge as low as 40°F (4°C).

Rainfall amounts differ greatly throughout the country. In the desert region, less than 4 inches (10 centimeters) fall each year. In the Sahelian region, rainfall can range from 8 to 24 inches (20 to 61 cm) during the year. In the southern grasslands, known as the Sudanian region, rainfall amounts range from 24 to 67 inches (61 to 170 cm) each year.

BAMAKO, THE CAPITAL

Bamako, Mali's capital city, is located on the Niger River in the southwestern corner of the country. More than 2.7 million people live in Bamako, around 13 percent of the population of the entire country. Its population has grown rapidly in recent years as people have left their rural homes. Drought has pushed people off the land, and they often flock to cities looking for work. Bamako

The center of Bamako is home to a large market square where people from all over the city come to buy and sell food, crafts, and other goods.

began its modern life in 1908, when it became the capital of French Sudan during the colonial era.

Today, Bamako is Mali's most modern city and a very charming place. It combines aspects of its African heritage with a strong touch of French culture, the result of its previous colonization. The Niger River runs right through the city, and there are bridges that connect the northern and southern parts. Thanks to a railway built in the early 1900s, Bamako is Mali's commercial center due to its accessibility and infrastructure. It has an international airport as well as a train and bus station. The city is situated at the foot of the Manding Mountains.

Mopti is a sprawling center of trade in Mali. The Niger River makes it easy for merchants to transport their goods into the heart of the city.

At the Grand Marché (main market), the people of Bamako buy their household goods as well as clothing. There are also shops in Bamako where people buy items used in traditional medicine. Many of these items are animal parts that are thought to cure illnesses. They are very expensive for the average Malian, but they are very popular.

PORTS IN MOPTI

The city of Mopti is situated almost exactly in the center of Mali. It is often called the Venice of Africa because it contains a series of dykes and canals that date back several hundred years. It began as a fishing village. Today, it is home to more than 114,000 people. Mopti is also known as one of the trading centers of Mali because of its important position on Mali's principal river. Mopti has an arts and crafts market where one can find crafts from all over Mali. Here, where pirogues and larger boats dock, goods produced in the region, as well as imported goods, may be found.

Since the 14th century, most of the buildings in Djenné have been made of mud. It is an incredibly durable material but requires regular maintenance and remudding.

HISTORIC CITIES

Some of the most historic and mysterious places in the world, including Timbuktu and Djenné, are found in Mali. Though the town of Djenné (jen-NAY) has a small population of just 33,000, it is an extremely important place in Mali and in the Muslim world. It once was known as one of the two most important places of Islamic learning, along with Timbuktu. Djenné is a special place in Mali today because it is the site of a remarkable piece of architecture: the Great Mosque. It is the largest mud, or adobe, structure in the world.

The mosque is also the site of one of the most lively and important markets in Mali. Every Monday, thousands of traders and customers gather right in front of the mosque, and a lively exchange begins. This is a market meant for

Malians. The goods are household items, not souvenirs, but the market itself is considered a sight worth seeing.

In 1988, Djenné was named a World Heritage Site by the United Nations Educational, Scientific and Cultural Organization (UNESCO). This gives the city the means to preserve, maintain, and protect its ancient buildings. It shows that the entire world recognizes the importance of this town, and that is a great honor for Mali. The United States has contributed funds specifically to help preserve Djenné's important, historic buildings.

INTERNET LINKS

www.doe.virginia.gov/instruction/history/mali/geography
This page from the Virginia Department of Education details Mali's natural geography and its impact on Malian culture.

www.worldatlas.com/articles/the-biggest-cities-in-mali.html
This article gives overviews of some of Mali's largest cities.

HISTORY

Before the Dogon arrived, the Tellem people built cities into the side of the Bandiagara Escarpment.

THE HISTORY OF MALI IS MARKED BY the rise and fall of great empires and kingdoms. These empires controlled complex trade networks that moved goods over the Sahara, as well as east and west by the Niger River. Around the year 500 CE, the Ghana empire grew by creating trade routes for iron, copper, and gold. From around 1230 to 1600 CE, the Mali empire rose to power and became even larger. It shaped the culture of West Africa and strengthened Islam in the region. The cities of these empires were great centers of learning. They gave a place for scholars to study law, history, and astronomy, and were famous for their medicine.

From the late 1500s until 1892, Mali was broken up into smaller kingdoms and groups. These kingdoms were made up of different cultures, mostly practicing Islam or holding traditional African beliefs. In 1892, France took control of Mali, and by 1898, it had taken the cities of Timbuktu and Gao. For 60 years, Mali would be completely controlled by France

2

In 1927, human skeletal remains dating back to 5000 BCE were found in the Sahara in Mali.

before gaining independence in 1960. A multiparty democracy was created, but struggles for power and military takeovers in Mali continue to this day.

THE MALI EMPIRE

A man named Sundiata was the first leader of the Mali empire. It is said that he was one of 12 royal brothers. According to legend, the ruler of the neighboring state of Kaniaga murdered all of Sundiata's brothers but spared him because he was sickly and near death. By the year 1235, Sundiata had established the Mali empire. He conquered nearby territory, including Kumbi, the former capital of Ghana. This created even more trade routes for gold and salt.

Under Sundiata, the empire of Mali began to grow. Sundiata took the title Mansa, or King of Kings. He ruled until his death in 1255. He was able to control many different cultures in the region. His empire included the goldfields of Buré and Bumbuk, the salt mines of Taghaza, and the important cities of Timbuktu, Djenné, and Gao. Sundiata profited from all the farming and resources in the region. He was given tribute, similar to a tax, by people throughout the area. Most of the material goods that traveled through the empire were taxed. The Mali empire ruled over 20 million people at its height and had roughly 400 cities.

MANSA MUSA EXPANDS

Mali grew even stronger in the next century, during the reign of Kankan Musa, also known as Mansa Musa. He ruled from 1312 to 1337 and expanded the vast regions of the Inland Niger Delta and the important cities of Timbuktu and Gao. Mansa Musa was an exceptionally successful ruler. He ruled the large territory by dividing it into more manageable regions called provinces. He had a massive army that kept the peace and controlled the profitable trade routes.

Mansa Musa was inspired after traveling to other Muslim nations, and he brought home books and scholars to Mali. During this period, Timbuktu became famous around the world as a center of learning, with great mosques and universities. Djenné and Gao were important centers of Islamic study. They attracted Muslim scholars from distant lands.

THE CITY OF TIMBUKTU

Tuareg herdsman founded Timbuktu around the year 1100 CE. The city is located on the southern edge of the Sahara, 8 miles (13 km) north of the Niger River. The city's location above the river made it a powerful trading center. There are different stories about where its name comes from. One claims that it is named after an old woman who was left to oversee the camp while the Tuareg roamed the vast desert.

Timbuktu rapidly grew into a center of trade and learning in the Mali empire.

The city attracted caravans arriving from the north. They began to stop there to water their camels. Merchants set up shops to serve the caravans. While shipments of salt were coming down from the north, shipments of gold were traveling up from the southwest. By the 15th century, the city's population had grown to 100,000, continuing to thrive long after the fall of the Mali empire.

As the business side of the city grew, so too did its religious and intellectual sides. Timbuktu became known as a center of Islamic learning. It had universities where scholars kept great libraries filled with books about medicine, astronomy, law, geography, and history. Scribes translated books by Plato and other famous people around the world. Families created their own libraries, with most of the texts written in Arabic, but many also written in African languages. The books remained in families, becoming part of the heritage of each new generation. It is estimated that Timbuktu was home to more than half a million books and manuscripts, many dating back to the 12th century.

ISLAM GROWS

One of the biggest changes that took place during the time of Mansa Musa was the establishment of Islam as the religion of the empire's rulers. Islam had been introduced by Muslim traders coming from North Africa and was practiced alongside traditional African religions. Mansa Musa wanted to show that he was an extremely faithful Muslim, like the rulers before him. In 1324, he made a pilgrimage to Mecca, the Muslim holy city in today's Saudi Arabia. He did it in an extremely grand style. It is believed that he traveled with tens of thousands of people, carrying an enormous amount of gold. Along the way, he gave away so much of it, he caused gold prices to drop in Egypt. The market for gold did not recover there for 12 years.

AFTER THE EMPIRES

After the death of Mansa Musa, the Mali empire began to weaken. New trade routes were opened up by the Portuguese, and the discovery of new gold meant that the empire no longer controlled most of the trade. The Tuareg,

THE MALI MANUSCRIPTS

Preserving the manuscripts of Mali is important for how we see African history. "The manuscripts talk about everything," according to Abdel Kader Haidara, a member of an ancient Timbuktu family who has inherited his family's impressive collection of books. Some of the collection is 850 years old. "There are copies of the Koran and hadiths (sayings of the Prophet Muhammad) as well as sermons and explanations of Islamic law. The books also discuss astronomy, mathematics, medicine, and geography. There are manuscripts of contracts, commercial records, and decrees that show how conflicts were resolved. They are changing the way people think about Africa, and Africans, because they prove that there was a literate culture in place a long time ago. Even though Timbuktu lost its position as a place of scholarly learning, its history was just waiting to be discovered by the outside world."

The manuscripts left in Timbuktu continue to be read by scholars today.

whose nomadic way of life made them more difficult to rule than the settled farmers, rebelled against the government. They raided Timbuktu, which was in the northernmost reaches of the empire. By the mid-15th century, the Mali empire had been taken over by the Songhai empire that had already been established around Gao. Then, the land was invaded by the Moroccan army from the north in 1591. Although the Moroccans broke up the existing government, they were not able to rule such an enormous area. Their homeland, in the north of Africa, was separated from Mali by the forbidding Sahara. Smaller kingdoms and dynasties began to battle for power.

In the late 17th century, a man known as Bitòn Coulibaly was born. He is credited with establishing the Bambara empire in Ségou, where he became head of the Tòn, an organization for young men. With these warriors, he overpowered other chiefs in the region and grew the Bambara empire. His army was fearsome to his rivals. It is estimated that he had 1,000 men, as well as a navy of war canoes, to fight battles and patrol the Niger River. Coulibaly captured people to sell to the Europeans and other nations. After his death, a formerly enslaved person named Ngolo Diarra continued to rule the empire.

COLONIAL RULE

From 1591 to 1892, the region was left without a large central government. Smaller powers rose up, including the Bambara empire, the kingdom of Kaarta, the Toucouleur empire, and several others. These kingdoms fought among themselves until outside nations began to conquer Africa and divide it up for its resources during the late 1800s. A battle for control was being fought by France and the remaining kingdoms in West Africa. France had used its outposts in Senegal to expand into the region, and by the 1890s, the French had gained total control of modern-day Mali, known then as French Sudan.

The French colonial period was marked by two different ways of governing. In the early 1900s, the French tried a policy of assimilation. This encouraged Africans to be educated in French culture so they would be more closely controlled by France. This shifted to a policy called association, in which the Africans were encouraged to merge their own culture with French culture. Throughout French rule, they would allow the practice of Islam and the use of Arabic, but they did not want them to spread further. The introduction of the French language had a long-lasting effect on the nation. To this day, French is the official language of Mali. However, the Bambara language is still widely used.

Over the next 60 years, the French ruled over Mali. In West Africa, they controlled eight territories including Mali: Dahomey (the modern-day nation of Benin), French Guinea (now called Guinea), Côte d'Ivoire, Mauritania, Niger, Senegal, and Upper Volta (now the nation of Burkina Faso). This entire region

was ruled by a governor-general. Between World War I (1914—1918) and World War II (1939—1945), opposition to French colonial rule grew. This opposition was nurtured in trade unions. These organizations, especially the teachers' union, gave Malians a place to meet and exchange views. One of the most important of these unions was the Sudanese Union, led by Modibo Keita, who would lead Mali to independence.

Mali has maintained respect for its military throughout its history. In 1924, this statue was erected to honor the African troops who fought in World War I.

MODERN INDEPENDENCE

French control ended in 1960, when the region now called the Republic of Mali became fully independent. Its first president was Modibo Keita. He began to steer Mali on a dramatically different course. He believed in socialism, a system in which the government directs the economy. He ruled by military force, pushing his policies forward even against the people's wishes. By 1967, some of his new policies started to hurt the economy. There were shortages of

consumer products, especially food. Within a few years, he had no choice but to make a deal with France, the former colonial ruler, to accept aid if he changed his policies. His own political party members were furious about this and tried to force their socialist policies on Malians, who were mostly against them. The military officers themselves, who were being used to enforce the policies, soon revolted. In 1968, while Keita was out of the capital city of Bamako, they staged a bloodless coup. They seized power from the government and arrested Keita when he tried to return. This coup was headed by a lieutenant in the army named Moussa Traoré.

A ONE-PARTY STATE

Unfortunately for Mali, Traoré established a military government and ruled the country as he saw fit from 1968 until 1991. In 1979, he declared Mali to

Many visitors to Mali came as Peace Corps workers. In 1960, John F. Kennedy was campaigning for the presidency of the United States. When he arrived at the University of Michigan, he made a speech that electrified the students and ultimately led to the formation of the program called the Peace Corps. In his speech, he challenged students to "serve the cause of peace" by living and working in developing countries. Students, as well as older adults, enthusiastically took up his challenge, devoting two years of their lives to the program.

The Peace Corps program worked in Mali from 1971 to 2012, and from 2014 to 2015. More than 2,600 Peace Corps volunteers served in the program in Mali during those years. The program in Mali was one of the largest Peace Corps programs in Africa. It worked in many different areas of development. Its goal was to create programs that the Malians could continue on their own when the volunteers left. These programs included ones dealing with food production, water availability, environmental conservation, small-business development, and preventive health care, including HIV/AIDS awareness.

be a one-party state. His vision of a socialist country led to collective farms, trade with China and the Soviet Union, and the abolishment of the country's first constitution. Although he had come into office with a promise to return the country to civilian rule, he used his power to remove opponents to his military rule. He made sure that he and his party, the Military Committee for National Liberation, stayed in power by any means necessary.

POWER STRUGGLES

After he seized control of Mali, Traoré clung to power until the early 1990s. His government was marked by corruption—many people had been given jobs in the government to keep them on his side. A devastating famine in 1984 put even greater economic pressure on the country. Protests against the government and its policies continued to grow, led by students and trade union members. In 1991, the military put down a protest in Bamako. Official sources claimed only 27 people had died in the protest, but the locals claimed that hundreds were killed. Only days later, Traoré was thrown out of power

Mali is now home
to more than
20 political parties,
most of which
are represented
somewhere within
the government.

the same way he came into it, through a coup led by a military commander, Lieutenant Colonel Amadou Toumani Touré. Touré is known as the "soldier of democracy" because he turned the government over to the people after he ended the military dictatorship, which led to a multiparty democracy and Mali's first democratically elected president, Alpha Oumar Konaré, in 1992. Konaré remained in power until 2002, when he lost to Touré in an election. Touré would then be re-elected in 2007, only to lose power during great social uprisings in 2012.

THE FUTURE OF MALI

The people of Mali continue to break up into different groups based on location, religion, and political beliefs. In 2012 and again in 2020, the government was overthrown by military coups. In 2007, Tuareg rebels clashed with the central government to form their own state. Peace deals were signed and broken. By 2009, the government took control of the rebel camps, forcing them to surrender. In 2012, a new Tuareg rebellion took control of northern towns and declared independence. The Tuareg people continue to take control of cities and fight military groups but also still meet with leaders to try and establish peace.

While the long struggles inside Mali grew to a boiling point, so did the threat of Islamic extremism. Militant Islamic groups began to take advantage of the chaos caused by the Tuareg conflicts. The United Nations (UN) had agreed to work with France to offer support to Mali, and French troops once again entered the country. Neighboring nations and outside powers want to stop the spread of extremism, including branches of al-Qaeda, and operations still take place to drive extremists out of cities and towns. France still supports the fight against extremism in West Africa, and in February 2020, it announced it would add 600 more troops to the region.

In the summer of 2020, protests began calling for the resignation of President Ibrahim Boubacar Keïta, who had been elected in 2013. A combination of poor leadership in the face of terrorism, corruption, a weakening economy, and the ongoing COVID-19 pandemic made removing him from office seem like the only solution. On August 18, the military once again led a coup in the capital and forced Keïta and his government to step aside. Since then, an acting military government has been put in place with promises to return to civilian rule within 18 months.

It is hard to understand how a country can be so divided, but growth for a developing nation is never easy. A long history of empires, warring kingdoms, and colonial control makes things even harder for the people of Mali. Through all of the transitions of power, hope still shines brightly for the region. Peace talks among political parties and ethnic groups continue to find solutions for the problems of today. At the same time, scholars work tirelessly to preserve the rich history of Mali and to learn from it.

In 1990, civil war broke out between the Tuareg and the Malian government. In 1996, more than 3,000 weapons were burned as a sign of peace when the conflict came to an end.

INTERNET LINKS

www.ancient.eu/Mali_Empire
This webpage provides a detailed account of the rise and fall of the Mali empire.

www.bbc.com/news/world-africa-13881978
This article features an in-depth timeline of events in Mali.

GOVERNMENT

Mali's flag is green, gold, and red, the traditional colors of the African freedom movement.

3

MALI BECAME A CONSTITUTIONAL democracy in 1992. After the 1991 antigovernment protests and the removal of President Traoré, a transitional government was formed to draft a new constitution. The constitution spelled out the structure of the new democratic government. Among other changes, it provided for the separation of powers among three branches— executive, legislative, and judicial—and allowed for the creation of political parties.

Today, Mali is in the hands of another transitional government. Following the 2020 military takeover of the Malian government, a temporary president, vice president, and prime minister were chosen to oversee the 18-month transition back to civilian rule. Many countries and international groups condemned the coup and cut off aid to Mali to pressure the transitional government into returning the country to a democratic system as soon as possible.

Everyone 18 and older has the right to vote in Mali, although only 37 percent of registered voters actually vote in elections.

The Malian government headquarters are located in Bamako.

EXECUTIVE AND LEGISLATIVE BRANCHES

According to the constitution, Mali is a republic headed by a president, who is the head of state and commander in chief of the armed forces. The prime minister is in charge of government operations and is appointed by the president. A cabinet of ministers is appointed by the prime minister to help run the country. These positions make up the executive branch of the government. As of spring 2021, the transitional government is headed by Acting President Bah N'Daw, Acting Vice President Assimi Goïta, and Acting Prime Minister Moctar Ouane. They are supported by a cabinet of 25 members, 4 of whom are military personnel and 21 of whom are civilians.

The legislative branch has one house with 147 seats, called the National Assembly. Its members serve five-year terms. The legislature writes the laws

LE MALI

Seydou Badian Kouyaté, a politican and novelist, and Banzumana Sissoko, a noted Malian musician, composed Mali's national anthem, "Le Mali." The song is also known as "Pour l'Afrique et pour toi, Mali" ("For Africa and for you, Mali") and "A ton appel Mali" ("At your call, Mali"). It was written in French.

ENGLISH LYRICS

At your call, Mali,
So that you may prosper,
Faithful to your destiny,
We shall all be united,
One people, one goal, one faith
For a united Africa.
If the enemy should show himself
Within or without,
On the ramparts,
We are ready to stand and die.
CHORUS:
For Africa and for you, Mali,
Our banner shall be liberty.
For Africa and for you, Mali,
Our fight shall be for unity.
Oh, Mali of today,
Oh, Mali of tomorrow,
The fields are flowering with hope
And hearts are thrilling with confidence.

Africa is at last arising,
Let us greet this new day.
Let us greet freedom,
Let us march toward unity.
Refound dignity
Supports our struggle.
Faithful to our oath

To make a united Africa,
Together, arise, my brothers,
All to the place where honor calls.
CHORUS
Stand up, towns and countryside,
Stand up, women, stand up young and old,
For the Fatherland on the road
Toward a radiant future.
For the sake of our dignity
Let us strengthen our ranks;
For the public well-being
Let us forge the common good.
Together, shoulder to shoulder,
Let us work for happiness.
CHORUS
The road is hard, very hard,
That leads to common happiness.
Courage and devotion,
Constant vigilance,
Courage and devotion,
Constant vigilance,
Truth from olden times,
The truths of every day,
Happiness through effort
Will build the Mali of tomorrow.
CHORUS

Due to backlogs in the judicial system, unsentenced prisoners make up most of the prison population in Mali.

that govern the nation. It meets twice a year to debate and vote on new legislation. The former president of the assembly, Moussa Timbiné, was ousted during the 2020 coup, and the position remains vacant.

In both the executive and legislative branches, elected officials serve five-year terms, and anyone elected president is only allowed to serve two terms in their lifetime.

THE JUDICIAL BRANCH

The highest courts in Mali are the Supreme Court and the Constitutional Court. The Supreme Court is composed of 19 judges appointed by the Ministry of Justice. These judges serve five-year terms and are organized into judicial, administrative, and accounting sections to make sure that laws are being carried out properly.

The Constitutional Court ensures that the laws passed by the National Assembly are constitutional. It consists of nine judges who serve renewable seven-year terms.

The country's legal system combines two very different legal systems. Its main laws were inherited from France during the colonial period. Its other laws are based on ancient and deep-rooted tribal traditions. In the French civil law system, written laws are very specific. It was originally created to make laws clearer and to give ordinary people power. It was a reaction to the power of monarchs who ruled according to their own interests. The newly written laws made it possible for people to be treated more fairly. However, the code established the principle that a person was presumed guilty until proven innocent if the person was arrested by the state. It also established the idea that all male citizens were equal in the eyes of the law, but women were not considered equal to men. Fathers and husbands ruled over their children and wives. Today, most of the outdated parts of the colonial justice system have been removed, and Mali's legal system is generally considered progressive.

Customary law is based on tradition. It is most often used in rural areas. In customary law, people often talk their way through the known facts of a case and come to a decision that is most fair to all the people involved. Customary law also takes into consideration the tribal beliefs and practices of each group. It recognizes that in small village settings, it is important to come to a settlement that people can live with. It is, in many ways, more personal than the formal French code of laws. However, it also tends to be conservative and patriarchal, which sometimes conflicts with the code of human rights set down in the constitution.

ADMINISTRATION AND NATIONAL SYMBOLS

The country is divided into ten administrative regions and one district: Gao, Kayes, Kidal, Koulikoro, Ménaka, Mopti, Ségou, Sikasso, Taoudenni, Timbuktu, and the District de Bamako.

Mali gained its independence from France on September 22, 1960, and September 22 is a national holiday. This is an exciting event in Mali, marked with parades and political speeches. It marks the day that Mali broke away from a colonial power and became a nation. The country adopted its constitution on January 12, 1992.

The country's flag has three vertical bands of color—green, gold, and red. These colors were chosen to represent three aspects of Mali. Green symbolizes nature and agriculture. Gold represents the element of gold—the wealth of the nation—and red symbolizes the sacrifices made to gain independence. These colors were adopted from the flag of Ethiopia. Ethiopia remained free during the colonial period and inspired many African nations to fight for their freedom.

The seal of Mali features the Great Mosque of Djenné, symbolizing Islam, as well as the country's motto—"One People, One Goal, One Faith."

ELECTING OFFICIALS

Mali has enjoyed a democratic government since 1992, when multiparty elections became the rule. There is generally tremendous competition for

Ballots in Mali feature the names, photos, and party symbols of each candidate. To vote, people mark their ballots with a fingerprint next to their choices.

political offices, especially the presidency. In 2018, there were 24 candidates for president.

Mali uses a two-round election system. In the first round, all of the parties are represented. If no one party gets a majority of the votes, then a second round of voting is needed. With so many parties competing for votes, there is rarely one party with a majority of the votes. In the second round, however, only the top two vote-getters compete.

The last presidential election was held in 2018, with Ibrahim Boubacar Keïta re-elected as the president of Mali. The National Assembly election was meant to be held the same year, but it was postponed.

ELECTION OBSERVERS

Because Mali is still considered a young democracy, independent election observers are generally present during elections. Previous elections have gone smoothly and been deemed free and fair, but the 2018 presidential election showed what European Union (EU) observers called "irregularities." Although fraud could not be proven, Ibrahim Boubacar Keïta's re-election was highly contested by his opponent, Soumaïla Cissé. It is likely that this tension contributed to the coup that removed Keïta from office two years later.

INTERNET LINKS

www.cia.gov/the-world-factbook/countries/mali/#government
This section of the CIA *World Factbook* includes recent facts and statistics about the government of Mali.

globaledge.msu.edu/countries/mali/government
This page provides an overview of Mali's governmental branches, as well as a comprehensive list of its international organization memberships.

ECONOMY

Like seven other West African countries, Mali uses
the West African CFA franc as its currency.

4

REPRESENTING AROUND 80 PERCENT of the country's exports, the two largest industries in Mali are cotton and gold. Since the 1990s, the government has worked hard to stabilize these industries and Mali's economy. However, although the economy has grown, it remains a difficult task to keep cotton and gold production steady. The harsh climate and political unrest often interfere with the country's economic goals.

In 2019, Mali's gross domestic product (GDP) was $17.28 billion, but it remains one of the 25 poorest countries in the world.

Mali also has a number of small businesses that make products for local use. There is a soft-drink plant, a shoe factory, a flour mill, and a furniture plant. There are companies that make tiles, paint, farm tools, ceramics, and cement. Others are involved in sugar distilling, cottonseed oil production, and meat processing.

Traditionally, most of the wage-paying work has been done by men. Women mainly work in the home. This is slowly changing as more people move into cities. However, people are moving into the cities faster than jobs can be created.

Cotton grows in fluffy clumps called bolls. They are picked and processed into fibers that can be woven into fabric.

FARMING COTTON

For Mali, a nation in which most people live in rural areas, farming is the most important industry. Three-quarters of the people depend on agriculture to survive. Food crops are usually grown to feed one's own family. The surplus may be sold in a local market. For farmers, the single most important cash crop is cotton. A cash crop is one that is produced to earn money by selling it outside the country. It is estimated that 40 percent of the entire population works at growing or processing cotton.

Growing cotton is very hard work, especially if one farms the way most Malian farmers do. They plow their fields using donkeys and then plant the seeds. Then, they wait for the rains to come. They pray, perform dances, and then pray to the gods once more to send just the right amount of rain. The farmers hope they will not get too much rain, which can drown the young plants. The farmers also hope the sun will not be too strong and burn the plants, and that the pesticides they use will keep the boll weevils from eating up the cotton bolls before they are ready to pick.

After all this, if everything goes just right, they pick the cotton by hand because they cannot afford expensive equipment to do the job. They can barely afford to buy the seeds each year to start the planting process.

In the past, cotton has earned as much as $200 million a year for Mali's economy, but this figure has been under $100 million in recent years. Mali's cotton farmers face more problems than farmers in countries such as the United States. In the United States, farmers are given subsidies, or money from the government, for the cotton they produce. This means that even though it costs more for U.S. farmers to grow their cotton than it does for Mali's farmers to grow theirs, the farmers in the United States earn more. The price of cotton produced by U.S. farmers is guaranteed by the U.S. government, which pays them the subsidy. This subsidy for U.S. farmers does not depend on world cotton prices. The U.S. farmers do not have to worry about the price of cotton sold in the marketplace, unlike Malian cotton farmers.

CROPS ON THE NIGER

Water is the most important resource for farmers. In Mali, where the rain comes only during one season and sometimes does not come at all, it is not surprising that the best area for farming is along the banks of the Niger River. The best farmland is next to the Niger River, between Bamako, the capital, and Mopti. There is also good farming in the southernmost part of the country, in the region where Mali meets the neighboring countries of Guinea, Cote d'Ivoire, and Burkina Faso. There, in addition to cotton and tobacco, food crops such as rice, millet, corn, and other vegetables are grown.

As the Niger floods the land, it brings rich soil with it. This is vital for the farmers. The river is so full of soil, it has a nickname. It is called the "strong brown god." The brown refers to the soil mixed with the water. It

Malians grow vegetables of all kinds along the banks of the Niger.

is called a god because it brings life back to the dry land. In years when the rains fail, life becomes very difficult for the Malian people. Crops dry up, and livestock die. The people have to depend on food aid and hope the next year brings better rains. When the rains fail, as they did from 2016 to 2018, crops fail too. An estimated 1 million people needed food aid each year this drought continued.

Sorghum, wheat, and peanuts are also important crops for Mali. Peanuts are grown in many parts of West Africa and are an important ingredient in stews and other dishes.

RIVER MANAGEMENT

The fishing industry also benefits from the flooding of the Niger. Fish, including the Nile perch, use the marshlands as their spawning grounds. At the end of the rainy season, the waters that have covered the floodplain start to recede.

The fish do not have enough water to swim in and are easily caught by the fishers. The Niger River itself is a great source of fish.

Several dams have been built to control the flow of the Niger River. This allows officials to regulate the flow of water throughout the year. Two of these dams are located at Sotuba, near Bamako, and at Markala, near Ségou. Both dams are used to irrigate the local areas. This allows farmers to grow crops without depending so much on the annual rains. Even with the dams, however, farmers and all the people must still worry about droughts, when the rains fail to come. Other dams are used to generate hydroelectric power.

The Manantali Dam on the Bafing River was built in 1988. It supplies electricity to the surrounding area.

RAISING LIVESTOCK

For many people in Africa, wealth is counted in terms of livestock, especially cattle. People who have cattle have something better than money in the bank. They have something that can be eaten or sold to buy other goods. They have something that can multiply on its own and bring them greater wealth. For these reasons, when a family loses some or all of its cattle, it is a catastrophe.

In good years, when the rains come on time, there are millions of cattle, sheep, and goats in Mali. However, Mali has suffered many terrible droughts, and each time, millions of livestock animals died. During the drought that began in 1972 and lasted until 1974, it is estimated that 40 percent of all the livestock in Mali died. The herds started to increase again in the late 1970s, but another drought hit in 1983 and lasted until 1985. Once again, the herds were drastically reduced in size. Both of these droughts reduced the area in which cattle can graze, and many herders gave up entirely on keeping cattle. Most of the remaining livestock are now found in the Inner Niger Delta and in grazing lands to the north of the delta.

The encroachment of the desert has depleted the grazing region and kept the overall size of Mali's herds small. The largest concentrations of cattle are in the areas north of Bamako and Ségou, extending into the Niger Delta, but herding activity is gradually shifting southward, due to the effects of previous droughts.

Cattle are a small but important part of the economy, making up about 5 percent of exports. They are important because they can be used in place of money to trade for other goods.

Smaller animals that survive in the driest areas, such as sheep, goats, and camels, are raised in the regions north and east of Timbuktu. Camels are known as the "ships of the desert" because they are able to travel vast distances under the most difficult conditions without needing water.

CARAVANS OF SALT

Mali remains a country in which ancient traditions continue, even in the 21st century. Camel caravans still cross the forbidding sands of the Sahara to reach the salt mines at Taoudenni (also spelled Taoudénit) in the northernmost part of Mali. There, more than 400 miles (645 km) north of Timbuktu, deep in the Sahara, men cut salt blocks from the ancient lake bed where it was formed. The workers are the Bella people, a tribe who were formerly enslaved by the Tuaregs. Although free today, they continue to do this extremely hard

work. They live at the mine and work in unimaginable heat. They dig the salt out in large slabs that weigh 200 pounds (90 kilograms) each. Many have been working for the same Tuareg family for generations and do not know any other way to live or work.

Today, most Malian salt slabs are destined for refineries in Bamako.

When the camel caravan arrives, the salt is loaded onto the camels. Two slabs, a total of 400 pounds (180 kg), are loaded onto each camel for the three-week trip to Timbuktu. A caravan may be made up of hundreds of camels traveling together. They generally travel from October to March, moving at night because the temperature in the desert can drop 40 degrees from day to night. At the end of each night's ride, the camels are unloaded and allowed to rest during the heat of the day. The next evening, everything is loaded onto the camels again. The Tuareg person who leads the camel caravan has a vast knowledge of the desert. He can read the sands the way others read a printed

In order to allow the gold-mining industry to succeed, the government of Mali had to make major changes to its own rules and regulations. Before the gold rush, the government owned almost all the mining operations in the country, but it did not have the money or the mining know-how to extract much of the gold that was in the ground. In order to bring in new revenue, equipment, and mining engineers, the government agreed that it would own only 20 percent of any mining operations that were set up by outside companies.

The government also gave mining companies great economic incentives to start working in Mali. For example, mining companies do not have to pay any corporate tax for the first five years a mine is in production.

road map. The entire caravan of men and camels place their lives in his hands and in his knowledge of the terrain. He must know exactly where the next water hole is to be found because in the desert a mistake can be deadly. When there are no physical features such as rivers, mountains, streets, or buildings to help a person judge where he is going, it is very easy to make a mistake.

When the caravan arrives in Timbuktu, the salt slabs are loaded onto boats for the trip to Mopti on the Niger River. At Mopti, the salt is cut into smaller sections and placed in warehouses. There is a lively scene as the salt-laden boats arrive. Young women, many from the Bella tribe, carry trays of prepared food that they hope to sell to the boatmen and their passengers. From Mopti, the salt is distributed all over West Africa—particularly to Bamako, where the salt is sent to a refinery.

GOLD DEPOSITS

Mali is Africa's third-largest producer of gold. Multinational corporations such as Barrick Gold, B2Gold, and Resolute Mining operate 13 mines across the country. The gold-mining areas are located in the southwestern and southern parts of the country, at Bougouni and Kéniéba, near the countries of Senegal and Guinea. The gold is found within rocks, spread over large areas of land.

Some of it is deep within the earth, and some of it is relatively close to the surface. In order to extract the gold, the mining companies must first dig up tons of gold-bearing ore. Some of the mines are called open-pit mines because they are worked from the surface.

The miners scoop up the ore using heavy earth-moving equipment and take it to a processing plant. They make a huge circle in the ground, and when they have scooped up all the ore in that circle, they move to the next level down. As they go deeper and deeper into the earth, the circle becomes smaller, like an ice cream cone. Eventually it becomes too small to work this way. At that point, the mining company has to decide whether it would be profitable to sink a mine shaft into the earth and begin working the deposit as an underground mine. This is much more expensive, and not all gold deposits are worth it.

Panning for gold is a slow, difficult process. Although some mining is still done by hand, corporations have brought large machines to Mali to dig for gold.

At its worst, Mali's unemployment rate was 11.7 percent (in 2007). Since then, unemployment has dropped to 7.3 percent.

It is difficult to imagine just how big a new mine pit can be. The Sadiola mine in the western part of Mali, for example, measures 5,900 feet (1,800 m) long by 2,460 feet (750 m) wide. It produces between 400,000 and 500,000 ounces (11 and 14 metric tons) of gold in a good year. When it opened in 1996, the ore deposit was only expected to last 12 years, but the introduction of new mining technology has extended its life. The Sadiola mine continues to produce gold today.

Although industrial mining began in the 1970s, it was not until the 1980s that major gold deposits were discovered. By the 1990s, gold mining in Mali had become a large-scale operation. It was around that time that surveys showed major gold deposits that could be worked profitably by large-scale mining methods. Between 1996 and 1997, gold production in Mali grew from 232,808 ounces (6.6 mt) to 652,569 ounces (18.5 mt). In 2020, Mali produced 2,299,862 ounces (65.2 mt) of gold. Gold production will grow according to the world gold price. It should remain fairly stable at between 1.9 million and 2.3 million ounces (55 and 65 mt) per year.

Estimates of Mali's gold reserves vary widely, depending on which expert one asks. Some say Mali has 350 tons (318 mt) of gold reserves, while others believe the figure is as high as 500 tons (454 mt). This does not mean all this gold will be mined. Some of it may be too far underground to work, and some of it may be scattered over such a wide area that it is not profitable to extract. However, it does mean that Mali has a tremendous natural resource to stimulate the country's economy. Gold gave the economy a much-needed boost.

Although Mali's economy has benefited from the gold mining, that does not mean all the people of Mali are wealthier. The mines create environmental and human rights problems too. Although outlawed, the gold ore continues to be processed using cyanide, an extremely harsh chemical. The process also uses a lot of water, and that can be a major problem in a country where there is often too little water for farming. Mali has also come under fire for using child labor to mine gold. Human Rights Watch estimates that between 20,000 and 40,000 children work in mining in Mali, most of whom began working at age six. For these reasons, buying Malian gold is considered by many to be unethical.

FINDING WORK ELSEWHERE

For people who are looking for employment, there are simply not enough jobs to go around. In Mali, unlike in the United States and other countries, there is no government assistance to help support people who cannot find work. For a growing number of young men, the solution seems to lie outside the country. They feel that if they can reach a European country, they will find work, but this is far from a simple task. They face two major hurdles. First, they often do not have money to buy an airline ticket to take them out of the country. Even more importantly, however, they do not have visas to allow them to enter another country legally. In spite of that, many leave anyway, traveling by extremely difficult routes to try to reach Europe. Spain, which is the easiest European country to get to from Mali, has become a major destination for Malian immigrants.

They walk and try to hitch rides that take them to the coast of Africa in Morocco. There are two tiny parts of Morocco that still belong to Spain. These are the enclaves of Ceuta and Melilla. An enclave is a small piece of land surrounded by another country. During the colonial period, these pieces of land were fought over by European powers. For an African who wants to get to Spain, the first step is to reach Ceuta or Melilla. If they can step onto one of those tiny bits of land, they have officially entered Spain. However, their troubles have not ended. In a way, they have just begun. This is where the most dangerous part of the journey begins. Now, they must try to cross the Mediterranean Sea. Many people die in the attempt. Many others are caught and jailed before being returned to their home country. The Malians do not carry any official documents with them, such as passports, because they do not want the Spanish to know where they came from. They do this to try to avoid being sent back.

TRANSPORTATION AND COMMUNICATION

Mali's transportation system is very limited. Most goods, including salt exports as well as locally used products, are shipped on boats on the Niger River. There

River ports, such as this one in Mopti, receive goods every day from all over the country.

are 86,437 miles (139,107 km) of roads, but only about 26 percent are paved. These roads connect the major cities in Mali. Mali has a railroad that connects Bamako, the capital, with Dakar, the capital of Senegal. It is used for both passengers and freight. Modern courier services have set up business in Mali, including DHL, a worldwide carrier of packages and documents.

Because there is a lack of telephone networks in most of Mali, more people depend on cell phones than on traditional landlines. While there were only 228,000 landline telephones in use in 2019, there were 22 million cell phones. Many people own television sets, but there are more radios in use, and that is how most people get their news, information, and entertainment. There are more radio broadcasting stations in Mali than in any other African nation, offering 370 programs.

Some radios work using batteries and do not depend on electricity. Most people outside the main cities do not have access to electricity, although some have small generators. Some jobs are created through the sale of cell phones and providing cell phone services. Even selling batteries can provide employment. Many people set up small stands on the street, selling small quantities of batteries as well as food, clothes, and other basic goods. This is called casual employment. It does not offer much of a future, but for many people, it is the only kind of work they can find.

INTERNET LINKS

www.heritage.org/index/country/mali
This page scores Mali's economic freedom and details the factors impacting it. It also features a tool to compare Mali's economy to that of any other country.

www.worldbank.org/en/country/mali/overview
This profile from the World Bank gives an overview of Mali's economic situation.

ENVIRONMENT

The cliffs of Bandiagara, where the Dogon people live, are a perfect example of Mali's natural beauty.

5

N O ONE NEEDS TO TELL THE PEOPLE of Mali about climate change. The natural environment guides every day of every person's life in Mali, and no environmental change is clearer than the Sahara advancing across farmland that was once green. Desertification is one of Mali's chief environmental concerns. Generally, once the Sahara claims land, it does not give it back. So, after a drought is over, there is a loss of inhabitable land. This puts a strain on the remaining land. The extreme heat and dryness of the Sahara make the lands nearby drier and less able to support agriculture and livestock. At the same time, Mali's rapidly growing population needs more farmland to support it.

Mali is also facing many other severe environmental problems. Deforestation, drought, and lack of access to clean water threaten human, animal, and plant life across the country. Organizations such as the United

The Sahara has expanded by 10 percent in the last century, and 98 percent of Mali is threatened by its expansion.

Thirty-four
percent of Mali's
land is used for
agriculture, and
only ten percent
is forests.

States Agency for International Development (USAID) and the UN Development Programme (UNDP) are attempting to help by building irrigation infrastructure and teaching resource management strategies, but these missions are often interrupted by the country's political turmoil.

DEFORESTING AND ERODING

Desertification and the loss of agricultural land are not only caused by drought. In Mali, about 78 percent of energy needs are met by burning wood. Malians do not generally buy oil or use natural gas to cook their food. They chop down trees and burn them. It is estimated that the country uses 6 million tons (5,443,108 mt) of wood every year. Malians used to gather wood that had died naturally, but now that is not enough to meet the demand. Today, live trees are cut down too. Without trees for shade, the ground quickly dries out and becomes desert.

Wood is covered with soil and burned to make charcoal, which is then used for cooking fires.

WATER AND SANITATION

Being landlocked and at the mercy of a long dry season, water is scarce throughout the country. In urban areas, about 80 percent of Malians have access to clean drinking water, and in rural areas, only 70 percent do. Even less common are sanitation services such as waste removal and trash collection, which contributes to the pollution of water sources. Organizations such as UNICEF and WaterAid Global have stepped in to build public toilets and water points. These efforts are especially important in schools because children are most likely to die from water-related illnesses.

As the population increases, there is a need for more food, which means more livestock are being kept. The animals graze on the land, eating up the vegetation that helps to keep the soil in place. They also destroy the soil's ability to recover just by trampling on it. All of this contributes to exposing the land to the wind, and there is plenty of wind in Mali. It blows southward from the Sahara, across the Sahel, and onto the exposed land. The exposed land dries up and is unable to support farming.

However, Mali is fighting back. Working with international organizations, the country has become a center for the fight against desertification. It is a race to find solutions to the agricultural problems of the country while dealing with its enormous population growth. Programs have been put in place to improve the productivity of the soil and to train farmers to make better use of the land.

THE NIGER RIVER

Unfortunately, the rapid growth of Mali's population spells trouble for the Niger River. As rain falls on the farmland, it picks up sediment and washes it into the river channels. This slows the flow of water, and that interferes with the movement of the fish. Dams needed to control the flow of water also affect the environment. They change the nature of the river, often decreasing the flow of water to the habitats of the fish and wildlife around it.

One of the greatest threats to rivers and lakes in Africa is a beautiful but deadly weed called the water hyacinth. Like weeds everywhere, it seems to thrive even when conditions are poor. It can choke an entire water system. All the nations in the region must put their resources together to try to control it from spreading further.

Meddling with the flow of river water can cause lakes and ponds, such as this one, to dry out permanently.

WILDLIFE RESERVES

There is very little wildlife in Mali and few national parks to visit. The main park and the largest game reserve in Mali is Boucle du Baoulé National Park. It is located northwest of Bamako, in the western part of the country. Much of the wildlife that once lived there is gone. It is believed that hunting wiped out the populations of elephants, giraffes, buffalo, chimpanzees, and even

lions that once roamed there. Today, monkeys are the animals visitors are most likely to see.

There are other, far more remote national parks. They are Bafing National Park, in the southwest, near the border with Guinea, and Ansongo-Ménaka Reserve in the southeast, near the Niger border. The Douentza Reserve is the most interesting in terms of wildlife. Located in the dry area between Mopti and Gao, it has a population of desert elephants. They move around as the seasons change, seeking food.

Although many animals have been hunted to extinction in Mali, birds like this little bee-eater are plentiful.

MINING

When there is no more gold to be found in a mine, the huge pit that has been dug is an enormous environmental hazard. Some companies have pledged to

Although it is a huge source of income for the country, gold mining disrupts Mali's ecosystem and displaces the people and animals who live on top of promising gold deposits.

fill in these pits and return the land to the way it was. Time will tell whether this happens in Mali. The land there is already so fragile. It is possible that it will never again be useful for grazing or growing crops.

In addition, cyanide is still used to separate the gold from the ore. Cyanide is a powerful chemical used to extract gold from rock. It is mixed with water to create a solution. This solution is then poured into large tanks that contain the gold-bearing rock. The rock and the cyanide mix together, and the gold is released from the rock. All the rock is then dumped at the mine site, with the cyanide still mixed in it. Over the years, dust from these dumps blows over the nearby land, where it is breathed in by the people living and farming in the region. The people inhaling the dust lose their ability to breathe as the passages in their lungs become closed, leading to death. This poison also may remain in the soil for generations.

INTERNET LINKS

www.adaptation-undp.org/explore/western-africa/mali
This page from the UNDP gives information on the environmental issues in Mali, as well as links to find out more about the organization's programs throughout the country.

www.greenclimate.fund/countries/mali
This webpage from the Green Climate Fund provides links to news and stories about climate change adaptation in Mali.

www.unicef.org/mali/en/water-sanitation-and-hygiene
This program summary from UNICEF Mali discusses the sanitation problems that affect Malian children and the solutions UNICEF is working toward.

MALIANS

In general, Malians are friendly, welcoming people with a deep sense of cultural tradition.

6

With an average birthrate of six children per Malian woman, Mali's population is expected to double by 2035.

MALI HAS A VERY DIVERSE population made up of many ethnic groups. Most of the population live in villages, towns, or cities, although around 10 percent of the population is nomadic. These people do not have permanent homes. Instead of living in villages, they live in family groups in temporary shelters that are easy to move when they look for new grazing land or water. Mali's ethnic groups live in fairly well-defined areas, with very little overlap. However, as people are forced to leave their homelands and move into cities because of droughts, the groups are becoming more mixed. In spite of very difficult living conditions, Mali is a country of gracious, friendly, and hospitable people who share what little they have with strangers.

In Mali, people are born into different castes. A caste is a social class that determines a person's position in his or her culture. At the top is the noble caste, while blacksmiths occupy the lowest caste. This caste system was firmly in place before the French colonized Mali. Most ethnic groups in Mali divided people into three major categories. There were the free people, also known as nobles. There was the professional group, such as people who worked with their hands. The lowest category included enslaved people. Only within Mali's modern history has it become possible for someone to practice a profession that once belonged to a higher caste.

THE MANDÉ PEOPLE

The Mandé group makes up about half of Mali's total population and is believed to have originated about 4,000 years ago. Within that group are many ethnic subgroups. The largest is the Bambara, also known as the Bamana, who make up about 33 percent of the total population. They speak the Bambara language.

As the country's largest ethnic group, the Bambara culture has greatly influenced Malian society.

They are farmers as well as craftspeople and live in the southern part of the country, around Ségou and Bamako. The Bambara are famous for their masks and for their use of puppets in elaborate masquerades. The puppets are enormous, and the puppeteers actually hide inside so they can work them without being seen. This makes them seem very real and mysterious. Some puppets take the shape of mythical animals, while others look more like human figures. Songs accompany the puppets as they dance and move around the villagers. Sometimes people who are watching join in and dance with a puppet. The puppets represent human emotions and human qualities, both good and evil. These characters are well known to the Bambara people.

The Bozo people are a close-knit group.

The Malinke people, another Mandé group, also live around Bamako. Originally, they were famed as hunters and gatherers. The Sarakole people, also known as the Soninke, live in the northwestern part of the country. They are known to be good traders and craftspeople.

THE BOZO PEOPLE

The Bozo people are fishers who live in the central Niger River Delta and all along the river near Djenné and Lake Débo. Their temporary fishing huts are made from straw, and linguists believe their name comes from the Bambara word *bo-so*—"straw house." Time seems to have stood still for the Bozo fisherman casting his net on the Niger River even though there are high-rise buildings in the background. Fishers have been working this way for centuries. The fish caught by the Bozo are one of the most important exports from Mali.

Gathering in compact villages on the river banks, the Bozo make their homes from sun-dried bricks. Their culture is patriarchal, with the responsibility of fishing placed on the men and the responsibility of caring for the home and family placed on the women. Women also grow vegetables and tobacco to sell at markets.

THE FULANI PEOPLE

The Fulani, also known as Peul in Mali, are a cattle-raising, nomadic people. They move around their territory in search of grazing land and water for their livestock. As they follow their livestock, they live in small, round, grass huts. They value their cattle more highly than their own lives. Most of the Peul in Mali are found within 100 miles (160 km) of the city of Mopti. It is estimated that there are more than 2 million Fulani people in Mali.

The Fulani have high standards of beauty and put a lot of effort into their grooming. Upper lips of Fulani women are often tattooed. Fulani women are also known for their distinctive earrings. They are made of gold that has been pounded into very thin sheets. The gold sheets are then twisted into shape. The earrings can be enormous in size and are sometimes attached to a cloth headdress or supported with a strap across the top of the woman's head that allows the earrings to dangle at either side of the face. The Fulani are found throughout at least six desert nations of West Africa.

Peul women are known for their gold earrings, which are often larger and more elaborate than the ones shown here.

THE TUAREG PEOPLE

The Tuareg are a nomadic people who are very much at home in the Sahara. They are known as the blue men of the Sahara because the blue color used to dye their robes often comes off on their skin. They are descended from the Berber people of North Africa. In Tuareg culture, men cover their faces. It is not proper for a Tuareg man to show his mouth, even when he is eating. Tuareg women, on the other hand, do not cover their faces. During the 1970s, many Tuareg people were forced to give up their way of life in the desert because they could not find food for their camels. When conditions improved, they were unable to return to their traditional way of life because they did not have money to buy camels. They are now sometimes seen in Timbuktu, sitting in cafés. Those who still live in the desert seem to appear out of nowhere, moving smoothly across the desert sand on their camels.

To the outside world, they are one of the enduring symbols of Africa and of the Sahara. They are at home in the desert, making use of oases where they can find water. Though there are no roads across the desert, there are tracks, called *piste* in French. The Tuareg know the desert well. It is their backyard and has great meaning and variety to them.

The Tuareg have had a very difficult history. Their nomadic way of life gave them a sense of freedom, and they resisted being assigned to a particular country. The boundaries drawn by the French around 1898, during the colonial period, broke up the Tuareg clans by relegating them to different nations. The process of desertification has added to their problems because it has made previously marginal lands unusable. One of the biggest disruptions to traditional Tuareg life, however, was the droughts that caused them to give up their camels and livestock. Drifting toward the towns, they lost their connection with the desert. Once that was broken, even after the rains returned, many were not able to return to their traditional way of life. It takes money to build up a herd of cattle and enough camels to maintain life

Tuareg men are easily distinguished by their face coverings and blue dyed robes.

in the desert. The Tuareg say, "We cannot be separated from the desert. It is there that we are free in every situation."

THE DOGON PEOPLE

The Dogon, numbering about 600,000, live in an extremely dry and remote part of Mali called the Bandiagara Escarpment. The Dogon people have one of the richest cultures in all of Africa. They have a belief system that encompasses the entire universe. The Dogon are animists and believe in a great number of spirits that affect humans by either helping or harming them. The Dogon reenact the creation of the world through their ceremonial dances. Most of their dances are known as funerary because they are dedicated to their ancestors. The Dogon feel a very close connection to their ancestors and in particular to the souls of the dead members of their community. The Dogon wrap their dead in bark taken from the baobab tree. Once every three years, they cut the bark from one of the baobab trees in their village. Then, they allow the tree to rest and regrow the bark before they cut it again. During this period, they place a bandage on the tree to aid in the healing. It protects the exposed portion where the bark was removed.

About 1,000 years ago, Islam was making its way into Mali, brought by the Arab traders coming in from North Africa. The Dogon were committed to their animist beliefs and knew they would have to move far away in order to maintain their own faith. They fled to the Bandiagara Escarpment. That area is extremely isolated and very difficult to reach, helping the Dogon maintain their traditions and beliefs. Their villages are built on vertical cliff faces, making them safe from outsiders. Not only do they build their houses there, they also build their granaries, the buildings where they store grains. Most important to the Dogon are the niches in the cliffs where they bury their dead. For all the time that the Dogon have lived there, they have kept their dead very close. This connects them on a daily basis with their ancestors. It is estimated that there are 700 Dogon villages and many Dogon dialects.

One of the most important Dogon rituals is the *dama* ceremony. This takes place only once every 12 years and honors those who have died during that

As part of their religious beliefs, the Dogon circumcise boys when they are nine to twelve years old. The circumcision ceremony takes place every three years, but the exact date is decided by the head of the Dogon clan. The ritual is done in a special hut far from the village or sometimes in a distant grotto. In the Dogon village of Sanga, the circumcision grotto, a sandstone cave, is painted with red and white figures, symbolizing local families and history. These are used to educate the boys about Dogon traditions and folklore. The boys are kept in the grotto for three days. During this time, their wounds heal. Herbs are used to help in this. This is also the time when they learn Dogon ways. The circumcision ceremony is considered to be the end of the boys' youth. They are now initiated into adult Dogon life. After they are circumcised, they receive presents.

The Dogon are one of many African ethnic groups to also practice female circumcision, or the removal of some or all of the external genitalia. In Dogon culture, girls must be rid of what is considered their "male" part to become women. Little is known of the Dogon female circumcision ritual, but it is likely very painful and damaging. Many people outside Dogon culture believe female circumcision is a human rights' violation because of the immense physical and emotional trauma connected to it.

period. If the person who died was very important in the village, the ceremony will be longer and more impressive. The beginning of the ceremony invokes the making of masks. Then, over a number of days, the masked dancers descend from the top of the cliffs. Their dancing is dynamic and dramatic, and their costumes are brilliant and colorful. Cowry shells, once used as currency in West Africa, are sewn onto leather. Cowry shells are still highly prized because they represent something that is so very far away—the ocean. For some ceremonies, the wood masks can be attached to headpieces that rise two stories above the dancer. This kind of mask is known as the *sirige* mask. They are so well made, however, that the dancer can whip his head around, displaying the headpiece.

During these ceremonies, the masks are said to have been danced, and the ceremony is not complete until this has taken place. The Dogon put great stress on this. Otherwise, evil things can happen to the people. Their crops

The masks and costumes worn by the Dogon during their ritual dances are considered very powerful.

might fail or the village women might suffer miscarriages. Women specifically must stay away from the masks. They may view the ceremony from a distance, along with the children, but they do not take part. Children are too young to understand the true meaning of the masks and the ceremony. They will be taught about them when they are older. In some Dogon dances, men wear costumes that include bras, indicating they are taking the part of the women.

Their costumes are striking and sometimes frightening, which is what the wearers intend. The masks are meant to frighten because it is believed that they contain the souls of the dead ancestors. The ancestors can protect the

Dogon from evil spirits, but they must be honored. Because the masks are so powerful, they are made in great secrecy. Women are not allowed to see the masks being made. Women give birth to children and so are believed to have great power. It would be dangerous if such powerful people were present when the masks were being made.

INTERNET LINKS

www.cia.gov/the-world-factbook/countries/mali/#people-and-society
This section of the CIA *World Factbook* on Mali provides facts and statistics about the Malian people.

www.focusongeography.org/publications/articles/mali/index.html
This webpage features an in-depth look at Dogon society.

LIFESTYLE

Girls help their families by walking to the community well for water.

MOST PEOPLE IN MALI LIVE IN rural areas. Daily life involves farming, preparing meals, and taking care of livestock. Most of the objects people need for their daily lives are made by the people themselves. Women and girls are responsible for caring for the home and family. They make pottery and baskets, weave cloth, and walk great distances to get water for cooking and washing. They must also gather wood, pound grain into flour, and do most of the farming. These tasks, along with raising children, take up each day, and there is very little leisure time for a woman living in the countryside. Men and boys usually look after the livestock. This generally means walking great distances to take them to an area to eat and drink. Men also gather construction materials to build houses.

7

In 2020, 44 percent of Mali's population lived in cities, a significant increase from 35 percent in 2009 and a sign of the country's urbanization.

Living in urban areas in Mali is much the same as it is in other countries. People work in offices and socialize in bars. There are colorful markets and delicious street foods attracting natives and tourists alike, and dance clubs and movie theaters are popular nightlife destinations.

A FARMING NATION

About 80 percent of Malians grow crops for food and raise livestock. Some of them earn a living by fishing. All of these activities depend on rainfall. The land is very fragile; the topsoil can be blown away by a strong windstorm. The bushes and trees that hold the land in place are also nibbled away by the goats that can be found almost everywhere. Mali also has around 6 million cows that graze on plants for food.

When drought hits, as it does fairly often, all of these activities come to a halt. There is no vegetation for the cattle. There is no water for them or for the crops. The goats eat the last bits of roots in the ground, which allows the

For most people in Mali, farming is the only way to get food. Women carry grains such as millet back to their villages during the growing season to feed their families.

topsoil to blow away. Even when the rains return, it is difficult for the land to be used successfully for farming and grazing because the topsoil is gone.

In Bamako and the other cities, people must have other jobs to survive. Many people, however, still manage to grow vegetables on small plots of land, and some also keep chickens right in the city. This is likely to change, however, as more and more people crowd into Bamako seeking work. There will be less room for farming and keeping chickens. Buildings in the cities are often made with the same simple materials as those in the countryside. Mud or adobe constructions are common.

Families in Mali are not only made up of a couple and their children—uncles, aunts, and grandparents are also part of the family unit.

THE FAMILY UNIT

In Mali, especially in the rural areas, people live in extended family groups. These usually center around the husband's family. A Muslim man may have as many as four wives. Each wife has her own house, where she lives with her young children. Her husband will stay with her on certain nights. Young men who are not yet married live in their own huts. When they marry, they bring their wives to the family compound, and each couple then has their own hut. Often, the wives will cook together in a kitchen hut built just for that purpose. The elderly stay with their children until they die.

GETTING MARRIED

Marriage is at the heart of Malian life. Rituals and celebrations involve the whole family. The extended family, including aunts and uncles, who play a major role in their relatives' lives, take part. In Mali, a young woman marries into her husband's family. Marriage ceremonies are elaborate, even though most people earn very little money. There are tremendous financial obligations, especially for the groom. His family must give presents, either gifts or money, to the bride's family. This is considered to be compensation to the bride's family because they are losing an important worker. For a young herder, it will take about two years' labor to earn enough to make this payment. This certainly puts a strain on the couple, especially the woman, who must now work in the fields belonging to her husband's family so they gain a productive person.

There are three types of marriages in Mali. Traditional marriage is based on ethnic beliefs and rituals. Civil marriage is based on the laws of the nation. Religious marriage follows the laws of the couple's religion, usually Islam. It is possible to have more than one type of marriage. In the cities, people often combine two or even three of these types of marriage. By going through more than one ceremony, a couple can keep their civil rights, such as pensions, and also the privileges of their family heritage. At the same time, the couple honors the obligations of their religion.

Marriage takes place at an early age in Mali. In the countryside, the average age at marriage is 16. By 19, half of all women have had their first child. As many as 10 percent of women have their first child by the age of 15, an age when they could still be considered children themselves. The more children a woman has, the better her position in the household. Children are seen as helpers for the future. They provide labor for farming and cattle herding.

It is not unusual for a man in Mali to have more than one wife at the same time. This is allowed in the Muslim religion, and it is also common among the Dogon, who are not Muslims. Having more than one wife creates very complicated and crowded households. A family group may consist of 60 people. When a man has more than one wife, his children occupy different positions in the home. The wives also maintain very close ties to their own parents and other relatives. Over time, an intricate web of relationships is built up because the children of a man's wives are related to each other as half siblings, and they are related to other wives in a quasiparental way. Children and wives compete for attention, favors, food, and money.

Malian weddings are huge celebrations that involve the couple's entire family and sometimes whole villages.

CATTLE CROSSING

In a nation where cattle are so important, it is not surprising that there is a ceremony devoted to them. Each year, Fulani boys drive their cattle to grazing lands far from home to save them from the annual floods. They are away for a whole year, and when they return, they come back as young men, ready to take wives and their place in Fulani society. Their return in December is the occasion for a great celebration called the Deegal. At this time, the cattle cross the Niger River at several places, including the village of Diafarabé, arriving back into the area of Mopti. On the first day of the celebration, unmarried men and women dress up to take part in the Promenade des Jeunes (Parade of the Youth). People also decorate their houses for the occasion, painting the doors with white clay and the floors with dark clay. Girls buy special mats for boys to sit on. They will talk all through the night. All the people celebrate by eating, drinking, and dancing well into the night. The crossing of the cattle ceremony has been taking place since 1818, when the village of Diafarabé was founded.

EDUCATION ISSUES

Although Mali is a country rich in culture and tradition, it is poor when it comes to education and literacy. In Mali, only around 70 percent of children attend primary schools. The problem is especially severe in the rural areas, although there are efforts to improve the situation. Boys outnumber girls in schools by a huge margin. Among adults, it is estimated that only about 35 percent of the people can read, and again, men outnumber women in this category. This means most Malians cannot read instructions or work in any kind of job that requires them to read. It also means they cannot follow written instructions for taking medication.

Although there is a law that says primary education is free and required, there are not enough schools for all the children in Mali to attend. Another reason many people are not educated is that children in rural areas are likely to become farmers like their parents. If they are in school, they cannot work in the fields. Girls are also married at a very young age in Mali. Even before they marry, however, their parents require them to work at home or to work for

others as maids to earn money. Girls must help out with cooking and cleaning because their mothers are usually busy taking care of the younger children. With an average of six children born to each woman, there is a lot of work to do. Rural parents do not see any practical benefit in educating girls.

Another issue with education is the level of teacher training. In many cases, teachers have only a ninth-grade education and are not trained to be teachers. They are generally reentering the classroom they just left as students and are expected to pass along whatever they learned. There is very little to hold the students' interest. Because of the difficulty of teaching people in the remote, rural areas, USAID began a teacher-training program through a radio network. It reaches 85 percent of Mali's teachers and has helped improve the passing rate among sixth-grade children to 70 percent.

Young girls are often not given a chance to advance past primary school, but advocates for women's education are working to change parents' attitudes in Mali.

A RICH HISTORY OF LEARNING

Despite its educational issues, Mali has an rich history of intellectual pursuits. The best example of this is the manuscripts of Timbuktu, a collection of more than 700,000 manuscripts on topics such as art, medicine, philosophy, and science dating back to the 13th century. Through the centuries, many of the books were kept in caves by families in Timbuktu. Although this kept them out of the harsh heat, it did not protect them from termites and high humidity during the rainy season. In 1967, recognizing the need to preserve the materials, UNESCO provided money for a manuscript conservation center in Timbuktu. However, the project was enormous, and very little was accomplished over the next 30 years.

When Henry Louis Gates Jr., the chairman of Harvard University's African and African-American Studies Department, went to Timbuktu in 1997 to learn about the documents, he started a process to preserve the documents and make them available to more people. He suddenly had proof that Africans had a written heritage, something he had been told did not exist. Gates was instrumental in getting funding to start to restore materials from the extensive collection. Since then, more than 150,000 manuscripts have been digitalized and made available to scholars all over the world.

EDUCATION IMPROVEMENT

Organizations including USAID and Oxfam are working in Mali to improve the level of education and the number of children attending schools. In the rural areas, USAID built 1,740 community schools over a 7-year period from 1995 to 2003. The enrollment in school in those areas nearly doubled. At the same time, the program tried to improve the training of teachers and to distribute books in Mali's different languages. Many schools cannot afford to buy books without outside help. Although they distributed more than 30,000 books, that is just a tiny number when compared with the number of students who need them. Many children drop out of school because the books they have do not relate to their lives at all. The things that are taught are often still based on the French model, which has almost nothing to do with life in Mali today. The role of the Mali government in improving education is to accept all the aid offered to it.

Oxfam's program works to combat the dropout rate among girls by using a very different approach. They employ women from the same communities to visit schools and talk about their own personal success. This is called the animatrice model and uses non-professional teachers. They also talk to parents about the importance of educating girls in the hopes that it will stop them from pulling their daughters out of school. The use of local women is thought to be the best approach, since they have experienced life in those communities and understand the obstacles facing girls. Some of the groups they have targeted with this program are among the most difficult to reach in Mali—the nomadic and seminomadic people of the north, including the Tuareg.

ADULT LEARNING

One of the most positive results of the improvement in children's education is the desire of adults to learn to read. Since they must work during the day, they meet at night in classrooms that do not have electricity. An ingenious battery-powered projector was developed just for use in these dark classrooms. It was called Kinkajou, the name of a nocturnal animal with exceptional nighttime vision. Literacy lesson material was provided on microfilm so it could be used in the projector. USAID funded this program. Although Kinkajou is not used very often anymore, it was an important piece of technology in the early 2000s.

Many foreign-aid organizations and nongovernmental organizations are working in Mali in an effort to raise literacy standards throughout the population. These organizations know that with more education, the citizens will be better equipped to make good decisions about their lives. They can understand the choices offered to them, read about different ideas, and exercise free will. In a young democratic society such as Mali's, literacy is an important way to break free from autocratic rule.

HEALTH CARE AND DISEASE

Health care in general is very limited in Mali. Most women give birth without any medical assistance at all. Across the country, 1 out of every 10 children dies before the age of 5. The average life expectancy for those who make it

The coronavirus known as COVID-19 was first identified in Wuhan, China, in December 2019. By January 2020, the disease began circulating in Europe and North America. From there, COVID-19 swept around the world. In March 2020, the World Health Organization (WHO) declared COVID-19 a pandemic. The disease is characterized by a cough, fever, and trouble breathing, and it is often deadly, especially to the elderly and immunocompromised.

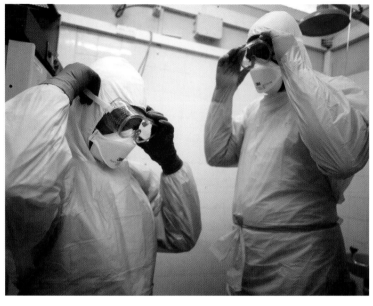

Researchers at the University Clinical Research Center of Bamako continue to track the spread of COVID-19 in Mali.

By April 2021, COVID-19 had infected around 10,500 people in Mali, and 392 Malians had died. Africa, overall, had a low infection rate, due in part to a quick response, a young population, the warm climate, and public support of measures such as mask wearing, hand washing, and social distancing.

into adulthood is estimated at 60 years for men and 64 years for women. Sanitation issues and malnutrition remain serious health threats in Mali, leaving people very susceptible to illnesses such as bacterial and parasitic diarrhea, hepatitis A, typhoid fever, and meningitis.

Malaria, a disease that is carried by mosquitoes, is one of the most prevalent illnesses in Africa. While malaria strikes people of all ages, children under the age of 5 are particularly affected by this disease, which is marked by a very high fever. More children under the age of 5 die from malaria than from any other cause. While medications to prevent malaria are extremely expensive and not widely available, there is a simple, inexpensive way to keep people from being bitten by mosquitoes. Bed nets, also known as mosquito nets, are treated with insecticide and then draped all around the area where someone is sleeping. The USAID program that provides these nets without charge has been a great help in curbing this disease. It costs USAID only a few dollars for each net. The insecticide in them lasts for five years.

Hospitals tend to be underfunded in Mali due to the country's poverty.

INTERNET LINKS

www.usaid.gov/mali/fact-sheets/mali-education-program-overview
This webpage gives an overview of USAID's current educational programs in Mali.

www.usaid.gov/mali/global-health
This webpage summarizes Mali's health-care situation and provides links to factsheets to learn more.

RELIGION

The Great Mosque in Djenné is a UNESCO World Heritage Site, meaning it has been recognized as a place of great cultural significance.

8

ALTHOUGH MALI'S CONSTITUTION guarantees freedom of religion, Islam is the dominant religion in the country today. Nearly 94 percent of Malians identify as Muslim, and the vast majority are followers of the Sunni branch of Islam. A small number of people, around 3 percent, are Christian. Half of them are Catholic, the other half Protestant. The remaining 3 percent either follow no religion or practice traditional animistic religions that predate the introduction of both Islam and Christianity.

Malians usually combine their devotion to Islam with some traditional religious practices, incorporating those parts that suit their African way of life. They do not see a conflict between proclaiming their faith in Allah, the Muslim name for God, and also believing in their traditional religion. This blending of beliefs has created a highly tolerant attitude toward other religions, and it makes it is easier for people from other religious groups to travel, work, and live in Mali.

Religious leaders in Mali are so popular that they are often able to fill stadiums with tens of thousands of people who come to hear their speeches.

ISLAM FOR MOST

Islam has a long history in Mali, dating back to the 8th century, when traders began to introduce the religion as they traveled southward across the Sahara. In the beginning, the practice of the religion was confined to educated people—rulers, merchants, and religious leaders themselves. The rural people mainly followed their traditional religions. During the French colonial period, however, the practice of Islam grew because the French administrators used religious leaders to help them control people living in rural areas.

Although most of the people in Mali are Muslims, the country is not ruled as a theocracy, which is a country where religious law comes before civil law. Its government continues to resist attempts by extremists to institute religious

The Great Mosque in Djenné was built in 1907 on the foundation of an even older mosque that was built in 1834. That mosque was built on the foundation of one that dates back to even earlier times—the 13th century. This type of layering is demanded by the Quran itself, which forbids a faithful Muslim from destroying a mosque. If, however, the mosque falls apart because of neglect, the site can be used to build a new mosque.

The mosque is enormous and is built from dried bricks that are formed by hand. A wooden frame helps support the mud bricks, but it has another purpose. Every year, at the end of the rainy season, the mosque needs a bit of renovation. The mud must be renewed, and to do this, a maze of ladders and planks is erected using that wooden support. The entire town pitches in to help with the remudding, even people who are not Muslims. As many as 4,000 people take part in the job. In this way, the mosque retains its shape and reenforces community bonds.

law. However, terrorists in the north have successfully imposed strict religious law in some communities, and Mali faces an uncertain future because of this power struggle.

In Mali, the Gregorian calendar, the calendar used by most of the world, is used for everyday purposes, but the Islamic calendar, or Hijri, is of equal importance. The Islamic calendar is based on the movement of the moon, so its 12 months add up to 354 days. As a result, Muslim religious celebrations do not have fixed dates on the Gregorian calendar, which is calculated by the 365 days it takes for Earth to circle the sun. Instead, holiday dates vary from year to year. Each month in the Islamic calendar begins when the new moon can be seen in the night sky. The Islamic calendar began in the year 622 CE.

THE FIVE PILLARS

There are five elements of the Islamic religion that guide everyday life. They are the testimony of faith; prayer; giving alms, or charity, to their community; fasting during the month of Ramadan; and making a pilgrimage to Mecca for anyone who is able.

A well-known
Malian saying is
"98 percent Muslim,
2 percent Christian,
and 100 percent
animist."

The testimony of faith means that the person must say, "There is no god but Allah, and Muhammad is the Messenger of God," in order to become a Muslim. This declaration is considered the most important pillar of Islam.

Muslims pray five times every day, kneeling and facing the direction of Mecca, the birthplace of the Prophet Muhammad in Saudi Arabia. These prayers are performed at dawn, noon, midafternoon, sunset, and night. People are allowed to pray almost anywhere, including at work, at school, in a field, or anywhere in public. One does not have to go to a mosque to pray.

Muslims donate a fixed percentage of their income to their community, much like a tax. They believe charity sanctifies and legitimizes the rest of the income that they keep for themselves. This money is used to support community members in need, as well as to build mosques, hospitals, schools, and other infrastructure to help the community as a whole.

Observing Ramadan is an important part of practicing Islam. During the month of Ramadan, Muslims fast from sunrise to sunset to honor the moment when their sacred book, the Quran (or Koran), was revealed to the Prophet Muhammad. Muslims may not eat or drink anything at all during the day, every day, for the month. Ramadan is celebrated according to the 354-day lunar calendar, so the season is always different. The pilgrimage to Mecca is a sacred duty, but it is required only of a person who can afford the trip and is healthy enough to make the journey. This pilgrimage, called the hajj, is performed in the 12th month of the Islamic calendar.

ANIMISM AND THE DOGONS

Before the coming of Islam, most Malians were animists. Animism is the belief that spirits exist in all objects. Every object has a soul and is therefore sacred and must be respected. This puts believers totally in touch with their environment. Ancestor worship is also common among animists. Today, many Malians continue to hold these beliefs while also practicing Islam or Christianity.

The Dogon people practice a particularly abstract form of animistic traditional religion. Their creator god, Amma, is considered all-knowing and all-seeing, but the Dogon ancestors are the focus of most religious practices and beliefs. The spirits that inhabit nature are personifications of good and evil, and the Dogon worldview is dominated by the struggle between opposing and complementary ideas such as order and disorder, sterility and fertility, and life and death.

In addition to their close connections to their ancestors, the Dogon believe they can predict the future. In every Dogon village, there is an elder known as a griot. He tells the story of the Dogon people over and over again, teaching the younger generation its own history. This is called oral history. When people do not have books, they learn their history from their elders. Griots can recite the history of their people going back through many generations. They are precious resources in their communities.

To look into the future, the griot takes a stick and draws a grid in the sand. He does this in the evening and then places morsels of food on the grid. That evening, the food attracts desert foxes that leave their paw prints on the pattern. The next morning, the griot and other elders gather to read the tracks left by the foxes, and from that, they predict the events that will occur.

Dogon elders use divination grids such as this one to predict the future.

INTERNET LINKS

www.worldatlas.com/articles/religious-beliefs-in-mali.html
This article provides an overview of religion in Mali.

www.youtube.com/watch?v=5cMU7ISwRoU
This short video details one version of the Dogon creation myth.

LANGUAGE

French is taught in Malian schools, although very few people are fluent in French as adults.

9

MALI IS A COUNTRY OF MANY languages. The official language is French, a remnant from Mali's days as a colony, but most Malians do not speak French. Instead, the most widely spoken language is Bambara. Bambara is used widely across West Africa, especially in trade, and it is also very similar to Dioula, another language spoken throughout the region. This makes it easy for Malians to do business with their neighbors.

Including Bambara, Mali has 13 national languages. The others are Bomu, Bozo, Dogon, Fulfulde, Hassaniya Arabic, Mamara, Maninkakan, Soninke, Songhay, Syenara, Tamasheq, and Xaasongaxango. These languages are spoken in certain regions, and most people speak Bambara along with their regional language. French is the language of the government, but most French speakers only speak it as a second language.

Dialects are variations of a language. They often develop in isolated areas where there is little contact with other people. In the Bandiagara Escarpment, where the Dogon people live, there are nearly 50 major dialects. Dogon languages vary so widely that some Dogon people cannot understand the language spoken by other Dogon.

Malian children are most likely to learn Bambara from their parents.

SPEAKING BAMBARA

The language spoken by most people in Mali is Bambara. It is estimated that 80 percent of the people in Mali speak Bambara even though the Bambara people make up only 33 percent of the population. The Bambara, however, live in the more urban areas of Mali, especially in Bamako, so they have had more opportunity to spread their language. During the colonial period, Bambara was used by the African soldiers in the French colonial army, so

Bambara is widely spoken in Mali. Here are some useful and common words.

welcome . . . . . . i ni chè
yes . . . . owó
no . . . . ayi
thank you . . . . . i ni cé

Numbers:

one . . . . kelen
two . . . . fila
three . . . . saba
four . . . . naani
five . . . . duuro

Food:

fish . . . . jègè
sugar . . . . sukara
rice . . . . malo *(uncooked)*, kini *(cooked)*
banana . . . . . . namasa
bread . . . . buru
milk. . . . . nono
water . . . . ji

other Malians picked it up. Because the newspapers and television and radio programs that developed after independence were centered in Bamako, where the majority of people are Bambara speakers, the language spread even more widely and rapidly. There is even an organization dedicated to spreading Bambara throughout the nation. This organization, Direction Nationale de l'Alphabétisation Fonctionnelle et de la Linguistique Appliquée (DNAFLA), was created in 1975. It also promotes the use of other Malian languages, including Fulfulde, Songhay, Senoufo, Dogon, Soninke, and Tamasheq.

For all these reasons, many people in Mali speak several languages. Many speak several tribal languages as well as French. English is gaining inroads,

In Mali, friends show they care about each other with elaborate greetings.

too, especially in Bamako. Dogon is spreading widely as the Dogon gain access to education.

GREETINGS

In hurried Western life, with everyone rushing around all the time, people pay little attention to the way they greet people. Giving a quick "Hello, how are you?" without waiting for an answer is normal. In Africa, however, people take time to greet each other and even go through an elaborate ritual that shows they really care about each other. Among the Dogon, for example, the ritual remains an important part of the culture. It begins as two people approach each other. Long before they are actually standing close together, they call out questions about the person's health and then about their family, parents, and even animals. Each question is answered. The other person goes through the same questions, and they are answered as well. All the while, they have been walking closer together and then even passing each other, but they keep up the exchange. The answers may be ritualistic, but the people acknowledge each other in a very important way. It is particularly important to bring up the spouse and children and then the parents in the greeting to show the importance of one's relatives.

Although Bambara is spoken throughout all of Mali, it is not spoken in any of Mali's neighboring countries.

INTERNET LINKS

translatorswithoutborders.org/language-data-for-mali
This webpage gives an overview of the languages spoken in Mali and features a map of where certain languages are spoken throughout the country.

www.youtube.com/watch?v=Vhxz9DSw2p0
This YouTube video features natives and visitors speaking the Bambara language.

ARTS

Building and maintaining an adobe house is an artform in itself. Craftspeople also take pride in making beautiful details such as these keyhole windows.

10

MALI IS PARTICULARLY RICH IN cultures that express themselves through music, architecture, crafts, and dance. Fragments of textiles found in caves on the Bandiagara Escarpment show that this art form was well established in the region by the 11th century. Each ethnic group in Mali practices its own unique expressions of art. In Mali, as in much of Africa, art is something to be used, not just admired.

TUAREG LEATHER

As a nomadic people, the Tuareg carry everything they need on their camels. They have become expert leather craftspeople, using the skins from goats. Saddlebags, which hold all sorts of useful items, including clothing, household goods, and food, are beautifully made. Women work on the skins, which are carefully softened and tanned before the intricately detailed decoration work begins. The Tuareg color bits of leather and then press these precise geometric shapes into the leather background. One of their techniques involves stitching that is used to create patterns on the leather. They add fringes of leather to the bottoms of leather panels. A woman will spend months working on one saddlebag, which is meant to last for years and years. It is placed across the camel, with a flat piece

"It's easy to take a photo, but what really made a difference was that I always knew how to find the right position, and I never was wrong. Their head slightly turned, a serious face, the position of the hands...I was capable of making someone look really good. The photos were always very good. That's why I always say that it's a real art."

—Seydou Keïta, Malian photographer

> ## THE BAMBARA HEADRESS

The best-known symbols of the Bambara people are the headdresses that look like antelope heads, with great antlers that are carved from wood. These represent a legendary or mythical figure, Tyi Wara. The Bambara believe that they learned how to farm, and particularly how to plant maize (corn), from Tyi Wara. During the important planting and harvesting seasons, ceremonies are held in which the antelope headdresses are worn by dancers. The Bambara also craft masks using the antelope symbol for their initiation rites. These symbols are very powerful in the Bambara culture.

of leather connecting the two bags. The bags hang down on either side of the camel, within easy reach of the rider if they need something. The same technique is used to make carrying cases for the Quran, the Muslim holy book, and for small purses worn on a long cord hanging around the neck.

Tuareg purses are particularly intriguing. The case is in two parts: The inner part is open at one end and holds the treasured items. The outer part is made to slide along the cord and cover the inner case completely, hiding the contents and making it impossible for a thief to take something out without the wearer noticing it. They are as beautiful as they are practical and are one of the most popular items visitors look to purchase when visiting Mali.

The Tuareg make their camel saddles from wood, leather, and bits of metal. Like the saddlebags, the saddle itself is decorated, colored, and embellished all over. The front and back of the saddle are very high to give support to the rider.

MUD CLOTH

Many ideas and objects have come from Africa, often without other people knowing their origin. Many of people have worn the beautiful material known as Mali cloth or mud cloth without knowing where it came from. The Bambara name for mud cloth is *bògòlanfini* (bo-ho-lahn-FEE-nee). The word *bogo* means "earth" or "mud," *lan* means "with," and *fini* means "cloth" in the Bambara language, translating literally to "mud cloth" or "cloth with mud."

Bògòlanfini is a special craft of the Bambara people. It is made by an ancient technique that requires a great deal of handwork as well as artistic ability and knowledge of the Bambara culture. The cloth is usually coarse and is made from cotton that is locally grown, hand spun, and then worked on a hand loom. Traditionally, men weave the cloth strips, usually about 6 inches (15 cm) wide. Once the strips are woven, they are sewn together to make a panel. This is usually about 3 feet (1 m) wide and 5 feet (1.5 m) long.

Once the plain cloth panel has been completed, it is turned over to the women, who create the intricate patterns from dyes that are made of fermented mud. These patterns and the techniques used to create them are a family affair. Mothers have passed the knowledge down to their daughters,

Artists use fermented mud to dye patterns onto handmade cotton fabric.

generation after generation. The patterns are more than decorative. They are symbols that can be read to reveal Bambara history and beliefs. Some of the motifs are very specific, such as drums or houses, animals or towns. Some are more symbolic and are harder for an outsider to read. The artist repeats the symbols over and over, enclosing them within geometric shapes on the cloth. All the symbols taken together create their own pattern, and no two pieces of mud cloth are exactly alike.

Traditionally, the cloth was worn only for special occasions, such as Bambara women's initiation ceremonies. Hunters were allowed to wear garments made of mud cloth because it was believed the cloth was so powerful, it would protect them during the hunt.

Today, the tradition is being kept alive in special associations, including the Boutique des Femmes (Women's Shop) in Ségou. The association brings together women and girls who share their skills. The older women have the chance to pass along their knowledge to the girls, who learn a useful skill.

Another group, the Maison des Jeunes (Youth Club) in Bamako, offers workshops. This club is designed to offer young people a place to gather and learn a skill, rather than just hanging around the streets of the capital. With these skills, they can earn money by selling the crafts they make.

INSTRUMENTS

Thanks to its different ethnic groups and their own unique histories, Mali has a rich musical tradition. The best-known musical instrument is the djembe drum. The djembe drum is made of hardwood with goatskin stretched over the top to form the drumming surface. Leather cords are used to secure the goatskin and are often laced in an attractive geometric pattern.

The djembe drum is usually held between the legs, with the drummer sitting down. It allows the drummer to bring out a rich variety of tones and is often used by storytellers. It also provides rhythms for dancers. The sound travels very well, which makes it useful for sending messages between villages. The villagers can interpret the messages from the rhythms that are played.

The kora is the most widely used traditional stringed instrument in Mali. Griots, also called *jalis*, use the kora to tell their stories, perhaps because it

is so versatile in the sounds it makes. With its 21 strings stretched over a long neck, the kora is a very complicated instrument to play. The strings are plucked with the fingers. The kora is played at important ceremonies, such as weddings and naming days, when infants are given their names.

Singing, dancing, and playing music are favorite pastimes in Mali. Every festival and ceremony is accompanied by some kind of music.

MUSICIANS

The best-known female traditional Malian singer is Oumou Sangaré, nicknamed "The Songbird of Wassoulou," her ancestral home. In her music, she tells the story of Mali, especially the problems that Malian women face. She sings about traditions that can make life very difficult for women, such as arranged marriages, and about the hard work women must do. Much of this material comes from her own upbringing. She saw how much her mother struggled in her own household. She conveys this in an unusually heartfelt manner, reaching out to the listener in a very direct way. Younger people feel she understands modern problems better than many traditional male singers. She is a communicator as much as she is a musician.

The unique sound of Ali Farka Touré combined the modern acoustic guitar with African ideas and a style that is close to American blues. When he first heard African American performers, Farka Touré realized that American music was deeply tied to its African roots. He was inspired by this music, and it found its way into his own sound. His music has been described as "sinuous," which means it winds around and around, drawing the listener closer. He was born near Timbuktu in 1939 into a northern Mali family that traced its roots back many generations and was considered to be noble. He began playing a simple one-string African guitar called the gurkel as a boy. Later in his life, he took up the acoustic guitar and adapted its sound to suit his artistic needs. He combined his life as a musician with a traditional Malian life as a farmer. Even when he became very well known, he continued to live in a village. One of his best-known albums is *Talking Timbuktu*. Farka Touré always dressed in traditional clothing, which contrasted with his very modern guitar. That combination shows that he was able to combine these two different worlds in his music. In spite of his worldwide success as a musician, Farka Touré always thought of himself as a farmer first and often left his musical career behind to tend to his farm. His village and his family meant everything to him. He died on March 7, 2006, after a long struggle with bone cancer. In many ways, he symbolized Mali and its music to a worldwide audience.

Tinariwen is a musical group that is considered the voice of the the Tuareg. It was formed in 1982 and led by Ibrahim Ag Alhabib. The recent history of the Tuareg people, their suffering during the resistance to both French rule and the Mali army, is told through their music. Tinariwen has been an important part of the Festival in the Desert. Traditional Tuareg music utilizes the shepherd flute, the imzad fiddle, and the tinde drum, but the threats to Tuareg culture inspired the musicians to give up these instruments and use the electric guitar, electric bass, and drums. They still use their music to tell the story of

PICASSO AND THE INFLUENCE OF AFRICAN ART

The artist Pablo Picasso was tremendously influenced by the African objects he saw. In Africa, art is not something separate from the usefulness of an object. This is true, for example, of Dogon masks, which are made for specific ceremonies. Picasso, more than any other European artist at the time, understood and felt the power and meaning these works had for the people who made and used them. He said that he "contracted the virus of African art" in 1907 when he visited the ethnographic museum in Paris and saw African masks there. He said he feared the power of the masks he saw and felt an intensely strong connection with the work. They made such a strong impression on him that he immediately interpreted them in his own work, starting with his painting Les Demoiselles d'Avignon (Women of Avignon). *He understood that the African artists exaggerated some features to emphasize the power of those features. This is why some masks have extremely large eyes or enormous mouths. That was done to communicate information to the person seeing the mask. The influence of animal masks from Mali can actually be seen in his paintings. Many art critics believe that when Picasso came into contact with African works, it changed the entire direction of modern art.*

the Tuareg very much the way the Dogon griots use music and storytelling to relate the history of the Dogon people. Protest songs are at the heart and soul of Tinariwen's lyrics.

In 2006, Tinariwen performed at a remarkable concert in New York City's Symphony Space Theater. When the concert began, all the singers wore traditional *tagilmusts*, headdresses made of cloth that protect the wearer from wind and sun, entirely covering their faces except for their eyes. These wraps loosened a bit during the first half of the program. The New York audience followed every song with enthusiasm, and it was clear that though they could not understand the words Tinariwen sang, they understood their spirit. In the second half of the program, the tagilmusts began to unwind more and more, and by the end of the program, one of the performers had taken his off entirely. This was a tremendous sign of acceptance. He felt at home on this stage in this big city as he sang about his homeland, across the ocean.

Gold Malian jewelry is a favorite among tourists.

GOLDSMITHING

In ancient times, the goldsmiths of Bamako were well known. Since Mali had a ready source of gold, the smiths learned to make beautiful objects from the precious metal. In recent years, the gold market at Bamako has become a favorite place for visitors. Malian gold jewelry takes its inspiration from mythology as well as from plants and animals. Gold is a very soft metal that can be worked by hand. Goldsmithing techniques are ancient and do not require modern equipment or even electricity. The metal can be engraved, hammered, or flattened using simple tools. The goldsmith can heat the metal using a bellow made of goatskin. Because gold has been mined in Mali for so long, the goldsmiths have a lot of experience in working with the metal and in creating beautiful jewelry that reflects the cultures of Mali.

DOGON GRANARIES

The Dogon make everything they use in their daily lives, including their houses and the granaries that hold their supplies of grain. The granaries are built on stilts to protect the maize and millet from insects. Each granary has a small opening cut into the wall. This opening is closed with a carved wooden door. Often, the carving depicts figures of ancestors. The door latch is very well made. A piece of wood fitted out with pins that form the locking device slides into place. A key made from wire bristles is pushed into the holes to open the door. Dogon doors are often sold at craft markets. Although they are small, they are very heavy.

Dogon crafts, including granary doors, are made to sell at local markets.

PHOTOGRAPHS

Bamako is an important center for photography and is well known for its photography workshops and festivals. Notable among these is African Photography Encounters, which takes place every two years.

The most famous Malian photographer, Seydou Keïta, was born in Bamako in 1923 and died in 2001. He earned a reputation around the world for capturing life in his native city. In 1948, working in his tiny studio, he created his own style and documented local people in black-and-white photographs. Although the portraits were posed, they still have a charming and informal feeling to them. People are seen laughing and talking while wearing their best clothes. Those clothes varied from tribal dress to western business attire, some of it provided by Keïta. Many photographs took elements from both cultures and combined them in a totally new way. Keïta's photographs captured the period during the 1950s and 1960s and earned him his reputation. They are a remarkable record of life in Bamako during that time. In all, he left a legacy of 7,000 negatives, the film from which black-and-white prints are made. Keïta's contribution to preserving the art and culture of Mali is enormous because it shows the point of view of someone who belongs to that culture. In many other examples, we see Africans through the eyes of Westerners, but Keïta showed his own people from inside their culture.

The first major exhibition of Keïta's work outside Mali was in 1991 in France. The world suddenly became aware of this remarkable talent and the fascinating people he portrayed. In 2006, the Sean Kelly Gallery in New York showed his work in huge, beautiful, black-and-white prints. A foundation in Bamako preserves Keïta's work and allows people to study it. It is called the Seydou Keïta Foundation. Alioune Ba, who was born in Bamako in 1959, is the director of the foundation. He is also a photographer whose work was included in a major exhibition in Washington, D.C., called "Mali, Beyond Timbuktu," in 2006.

Keïta paved the way for a whole generation of African photographers. Two of them from Mali were included in an exhibition called "Snap Judgments: New Positions in Contemporary African Photography" at the International Center of Photography in New York in 2006. Mohamed Camara was born in Bamako in 1985 and now splits his time between Mali and Paris, a major art center.

His work has been shown in exhibitions in several European countries and in Bamako. Sada Tangara was born in Mali in 1981 and now lives in the neighboring country of Senegal. His work has also been seen in many exhibitions, both in Europe and in Africa. They are continuing the tradition of presenting a view of Africa by Africans, not by outsiders.

INTERNET LINKS

www.maliembassy.us/culture-art
This page from the Mali embassy discusses Malian art and provides links to listen to popular music.

www.seydoukeitaphotographer.com
This website features the photographs of Seydou Keïta.

LEISURE

Football (soccer) is by far the most popular sport in Mali.

11

ALTHOUGH THERE IS MUCH WORK TO be done, Malians are not without plenty of recreational activities. In addition to dancing and making music, people enjoy sports such as football (soccer), basketball, and wrestling. Card games and board games are also popular.

Malians like listening to the radio. Since radios can run on battery power, they are found almost everywhere in Mali, and there is no shortage of programs to listen to every day. In places with access to electricity, television and the internet are becoming more widespread, but the infrastructure for these services is underdeveloped. Most visual entertainment comes in the form of movies, but movie theaters are a luxury of city life.

FOOTBALL

Football fever runs high in Mali, as in most nations in Africa and around the world. Young boys play in the dusty streets and bare dirt fields, often with a makeshift ball made of rags or newspaper. Mali has 23 professional football teams. In Bamako, the football stadium holds 70,000 people. During important matches, such as the qualifying rounds to enter the World Cup, every seat is filled. Mali's national team has become an important contender among African nations. It earned the right to host

Mali has more than 370 radio stations and only 23 television channels.

Playing football in the evening before the sun goes down is a popular pastime among people who work all day.

the 2002 Africa Cup of Nations tournament, where it took part in the finals. In total, Mali has qualified for the Africa Cup 12 times as of 2021.

At the Olympic Games in 2004, which were held in Athens, Greece, the Mali Minnows (the national team) scored a tremendous victory. The team won a game with a 2—0 score over Greece. The Mali team had already beaten Cameroon, the 2000 gold medalists, during the African qualifying round. Two of the star players were Moussa Coulibaly and Adama Tamboura.

In an effort to get more Malian children involved in organized sports and to help them develop better health, a group called RTP (Right To Play) has developed a sports program for children as well as adults. The children, grouped into three sections (under age 10, 10—14, and 15—19), as well as adults over age 20 are brought together to play football and volleyball.

POPULAR GAMES

The most popular counting game in many parts of Africa is called mancala. It is also known as oware, wari, and bau in different languages and in different countries. Whatever it is called, it is played the same way. The board is usually made of wood with little cups or depressions carved out. The players use pebbles, seeds, or any small objects as markers. It is a counting game that is considered as complicated as chess. Players move from one cup to the next, adding and subtracting the markers. Men can be seen playing the game everywhere in Africa. Sometimes they just dig the little hollows in a sandy area and use anything at hand as the playing pieces. One clever man tore up

Mali is one of three nations in Africa with the greatest number of people taking part in football in relation to its population. Every town and city has a football team.

Young men play table soccer outside in the streets of Bamako.

A card game native to Niger, agram is often played in Mali and in many other African countries. The Malian variation is slightly different than the traditional version. The game deck is composed of the aces, kings, queens, jacks, 10s, 9s, 8s, and 7s of a standard playing card deck, minus the ace of spades. These 31 cards are shuffled, and each player is dealt 5 cards. To begin a "trick," the player to the left of the dealer plays any card, and the game goes around clockwise, with each player trying to match the suit of the first card. To win the trick, a player must play the highest-ranking card of the chosen suit. Unlike most card games, the winner of the round is whoever wins the fifth and final trick, not whoever wins the most tricks overall. There is no customary number of rounds—instead, the players agree on how many rounds they will play to determine the winner of the game.

some bits of orange peel to use. It is considered a game for adults, although children can play it too.

In the cities of Mali, there is a popular game that imitates a football match. In many countries it is called foosball or table soccer. Two players stand on opposite sides of a game table and move carved wooden players attached to poles back and forth, trying to score goals.

MOVIES

Mali has a small filmmaking industry and has produced some notable films. Among the award-winning Malian filmmakers are Souleymane Cissé, Cheikh Oumar Sissoko, Adama Drabo, Kany Kouyaté, and Abderrahmane Sissako.

In 2006, Sissako wrote and directed a film called *Bamako*. It was a fictional story, but it described many of the issues that concern Mali and Africa as a whole today. Much of the film takes place in a courtyard, where people go about their lives, while at the same time, a trial is going on involving judges in robes and wigs. There are many stories being told at once, and people walk in and out of the courtyard constantly. The film was praised for showing an African story from the viewpoint of the African people.

In Bamako, Malians have a choice of movie theaters to go to. Many movies are aimed at the French-speaking population. For example, people could see the latest *Harry Potter* film with French subtitles when it was released.

Such leisure activities as going to movies are reserved for those who have enough money to attend—and enough leisure time too. In Mali, however, leisure time can refer to time spent attending traditional ceremonies, such as weddings and other celebrations. In rural areas, where most Malians live, work consumes so much time that leisure time is a great luxury.

INTERNET LINKS

www.catsatcards.com/Games/Agram.html
This webpage provides instructions on how to play traditional Nigerian agram, as well as its many variations, such as the one commonly played in Mali.

www.ymimports.com/pages/how-to-play-mancala
This website gives detailed instructions on how to play mancala.

FESTIVALS

Dogon masks are found at many of the
cultural festivals throughout Mali.

12

MALI CELEBRATES 12 PUBLIC holidays. Eight are observed using the Gregorian calendar: New Year's Day (January 1), Armed Forces Day (January 20), Martyr's Day (March 26), Easter Monday (March or April), Workers' Day (May 1), Africa Day (May 25), Independence Day (September 22), and Christmas (December 25). The remaining four are observed by the Islamic calendar and therefore vary each year. These are Mawlid, the Prophet's Birthday (12 Rabi' al-Awwal); the Prophet's Baptism (19 Rabi' al-Awwal); Korité, the end of Ramadan and the breaking of the fast (1 Shawwal); and Tabaski, the Feast of the Sacrifice (10 Dhu al-Hijjah).

Mali is the only country to celebrate the baptism of the Prophet. Muhammad's birth rites are honored seven days after his birthday, which is traditional for newborns in Islam.

The Festival in the Desert has been chased from its home region by unrest, but the organizers of the event continue to put on shows all over the world.

Mali is also known for its festivals. These cultural displays bring people together for music, dancing, and food. Festivals strengthen community bonds, and they allow the various ethnic groups in Mali to share their cultures with their neighbors.

THE FESTIVAL IN THE DESERT

The Tuareg are so at home in the Sahara, it is only natural that they would hold their own music festival there. Between 2001 and 2012, the Festival in the Desert was held each January. When it first began, it was staged in Tin Essako, a tiny oasis town of a few hundred people located 50 miles (80 km) northwest of Timbuktu. It took four hours of hard traveling on sandy dunes and rocky tracks to reach it, and all the supplies had to be brought in. In 2010, organizers moved the festival closer, only a few kilometers outside Timbuktu, to make it easier and safer to get there.

The festival was a true Tuareg event. Everyone stayed in tents, just like the Tuareg, and in the evening, the temperature dropped nearly to freezing. However, the musicians and the audience—people from all over the world—did not seem to mind. It was primarily a music festival, with the best of the Tuareg singers, drummers, and other musicians gathering for a three-day celebration of their culture. It was also the one time of year that families from the most remote parts of the desert met up and exchanged news. The Festival in the Desert was intended to maintain the Tuareg culture and to help make it part of the world music scene. Western performers shared the stage with the native singers, but the songs of the Tuareg took center stage.

While most of the musical performances took place in the evenings, the days were filled with spectacle. Tuareg men raced their camels across the desert in a splendid display of riding ability. There were camel parades, craft shows, and discussions of events affecting the Tuaregs' lives. Women's groups performed tinde music, their traditional singing and drumming, during the daylight hours as well. This was the time for families to visit, drink cups of sweet tea in their tents, and enjoy the traditional Tuareg life.

ON THE NIGER

Rowing contests on the Niger draw large crowds.

In 2005, a festival devoted to music, crafts, and cultures began on the Niger River at Ségou. Timed to take advantage of Mali's best weather, this festival, called Festival on the Niger, is held in the beginning of February. The spectacular setting is the backdrop for a cultural festival that includes all of Mali's ethnic groups. The songs and dances of the Fulani, the Bambara, the Songhai, the Dogon, and many more are staged there. The arts and crafts expositions display textiles, pottery, sculpture, and jewelry. Visitors are also treated to puppet shows and pirogue races on the river.

In 2020, dancers performed with these traditional puppets at the Festival on the Niger.

In its first two years, the audience was mainly Malian, but as the reputation of this festival has grown, it has attracted an international audience. It is a rare chance to see so many of Mali's ethnic groups in one place at one time. Even the storytelling of the Dogon is included, something that is rarely seen outside of Dogon country. Because Ségou is so centrally located and is not far from Bamako, this festival is one of the most important cultural events in Mali.

Also known as Eid al-Fitr, Korité marks the end of Ramadan and the end of the fasting season. It is a feast day, and women spend most of the day cooking. Men go to the mosque early in the morning for prayers, and when they return, family and friends gather together for a grand meal. Gifts are given, and food is donated to those in need. No one goes hungry on Korité. When the feasting is done, Malians often listen to a holiday message from the president on the radio or watch it on TV.

Participants in the Festival on the Niger also have a chance to take part in discussions about the ecology of the Niger River and the threats to its future. In addition to celebrating Mali's rich cultural life, the festival gives people a chance to consider Mali's future and the role those cultures will play in that future.

THE FEAST OF THE SACRIFICE

In Mali, as in most Muslim countries, the end of the hajj is marked by the celebration of Tabaski, also known as Eid al-Adha. This is the most important holiday of the year for many Muslims. Tabaski celebrates the story of Abraham. Abraham was going to sacrifice his son to obey God's command. Instead, God told him to offer up an animal in the place of the child. On this day in Mali, Muslims celebrate by slaughtering cattle and sheep. They give away most of the meat to family members, friends, and the poor. They also invite people to their homes to share in a festive meal. To mark the occasion, people get new clothes. In some villages, these are sewn by the local tailor. Young girls run excitedly through the village, showing off their new dresses.

The women take the meat from the slaughtered livestock and make stews with sauce and vegetables. These are served with bowls of rice. Villagers visit each other's homes, where they are always offered sweet green tea. Muslims do not drink alcohol, so tea is a favorite drink. During the evening, musicians begin playing their leather drums. They work as a team, creating complicated rhythms. The women and girls dance to the beat of the drums. It is a wonderful celebration and a great break from the daily round of chores.

Bobo masks are elaborate and colorful.

PUPPETS AND MASKS

Both the Bambara and their close relatives, the Bobo people, stage annual festivals called masquerades. The people use puppets and masks to tell a story. The performances usually take place over a three-day period, with parts of the story being told in the afternoon and at night. Each age group plays a role. The puppets and masks allow the performers to express the characters they represent. By hiding behind the masks and puppets, the people feel free to represent mythical and symbolic creatures. Since the dancers cannot see where they are going, they are guided by a man ringing a little bell. Musicians playing intricate rhythms on their drums accompany the dancers.

For Malians, these puppets teach values such as tolerance, peace, and sharing. The puppets also allow things to be said that might be considered too harsh if they came directly from one person to another. They allow Malians to criticize their politicians in a safe way.

INTERNET LINKS

publicholidays.africa/mali
This webpage offers links to learn more about how and when public holidays are celebrated in Mali.

www.thefestivalinthedesert.com
The official website of the Festival in the Desert provides background about the festival and information about the artists involved, as well as videos and photos from the event over the years.

FOOD

Rice is one of the most important food crops grown in Mali.

13

M ALIANS TAKE FOOD VERY seriously, but they do not eat different foods for breakfast, lunch, and dinner as people in many other countries do. In Mali, most meals are made up of a porridge combined with a sauce or stew. Malians have been preparing dishes like this for hundreds of years. The great traveler Ibn Battuta wrote about eating millet porridge when he visited Mali in 1352 CE! The food does not vary much except for special occasions such as festivals.

An average Malian household spends more than half of its yearly income on food.

POPULAR DISHES

There are differences in the foods people eat in different regions of Mali, but some kind of grain is at the center of nearly all dishes. Stews usually combine several grains, such as rice, millet, and sorghum. In the cities, rice is the single most important foodstuff, but in rural areas, cereals, millet, and sorghum form the basis of the diet. Couscous is a popular grain. It is made into porridge and then served with a sauce made with fish, chicken, lamb, or beef.

Rice is key to the diets of many West African countries. Scientists believe rice was first cultivated in Africa in the inland delta of the Niger River around 1500 BCE, in the area that is now Mali. African rice is different from Asian rice in both flavor and heartiness. African rice is more resistant to drought, pests, and weeds, and it is more well-suited to a variable, uncertain climate.

In Mali, climate change and political conflict are threatening rice crops. Rice requires a lot of water to grow, but only 3 percent of farmland is close enough to the Niger River to use it as a direct water source. In other parts of the country, irrigation systems must be built and maintained to bring water to farms.

In the Niger River area, where fish are plentiful during the high-water season, people cook Nile perch, also known as capitaine. The fish can be cooked in many ways. It is fried, grilled, or baked, but one of the most popular dishes is a Malian fish stew.

Agricultural products such as sweet potatoes, onions, tomatoes, peanuts, okra, and spinach are all staples of the Malian diet. Sauces, stews, and curries generally begin with a tomato or peanut base, with various vegetables and meat added to create different dishes. Fruits such as mangoes, watermelons, and bananas are used for sweetness.

Sunday lunch is a special occasion, but only for those who have the money to buy the ingredients. A lunch in Bamako might be a dish made of fish, potatoes, fresh vegetables, and oil. A woman will spend the whole morning preparing this dish for her family. Since most people do not have refrigeration, they can only buy small amounts of fish or meat and must use it quickly.

Jinjinbere is a drink made for special occasions such as naming ceremonies and weddings. It is simple to make because the only ingredients are water, sugar, lemon, and ginger.

FOOD CUSTOMS

The people of Mali enjoy three cups of traditional strong, sweet tea after each meal. Tea is served in tiny cups and is poured from a teapot at a great height. Each of the three cups represents an aspect of existence—the first bitter like death, the second sweet like life, and the third sugared like love. It is not polite to refuse the second and third cups. The tea ceremony is a way of welcoming visitors and offering friendship, particularly among the Tuareg in the Sahara. Drinking hot tea in the hot desert has a way of balancing the heat inside and outside the body. It is also a great excuse to take a break and spend time with friends and family.

Because people eat with their hands, it is very important to observe the local customs. People always eat with their right hands, whether they are right- or left-handed. This tradition comes from Muslim rules regarding cleanliness and purity. Most family meals are served on communal dishes, so everyone gathers around, digs in, and enjoys together.

Serving tea is such an important cultural activity that it is common for men to join tea social clubs called *grins*.

INTERNET LINKS

www.whats4eats.com/africa/mali-cuisine
This page offers links to Malian recipes.

www.worldtravelguide.net/guides/africa/mali/food-and-drink
This webpage provides an overview of food and drink in Mali, as well as a list of common food items.

TIGUADEGE NA (MEAT IN PEANUT SAUCE)

Cooking oil
2 pounds (0.9 kg) chicken, beef, or
    lamb, chopped
1 onion, chopped
4 garlic cloves, chopped
Salt and pepper
5 large tomatoes, chopped
4 cups (0.9 liters) chicken broth
4 tablespoons peanut butter
1 pinch thyme
1 pinch basil
1 pinch rosemary
2 carrots, cut into large chunks
3 potatoes or sweet potatoes, cut
    into large chunks
White or brown rice, cooked
Sliced bell peppers, for garnish

Heat cooking oil in saucepan over high heat. Add meat, and brown it well on all sides.

Add onions and garlic, and season with salt and pepper, stirring until the onions have softened. Add tomatoes.

Bring mixture to a boil, reduce heat, and let simmer for a few minutes, stirring occasionally.

Add the broth, peanut butter, herbs, and vegetables. Cover, and let simmer over low heat for about 1 hour or until vegetables are tender.

Serve over rice, and top with bell pepper slices.

POULET YASSA

Cooking oil
1 pound (0.45 kg) chicken, cut into
    serving pieces
2 onions, sliced
1 chile pepper, minced
Juice from 2 lemons
1 tablespoon Dijon mustard
2 tablespoons peanut oil
Salt and pepper to taste

Add all ingredients except the cooking oil to a large, non-metallic bowl, and mix. Refrigerate and marinate for at least 4 hours.

Remove chicken, pat dry, and cook until well browned. Set chicken aside.

Heat cooking oil in a pot over medium heat. Remove onions from the marinade, and sauté for 8 to 10 minutes until they start to brown.

Add the rest of the marinade and the chicken to the pot, reduce heat to medium-low, and simmer for 30 to 40 minutes.

Serve with rice or couscous.

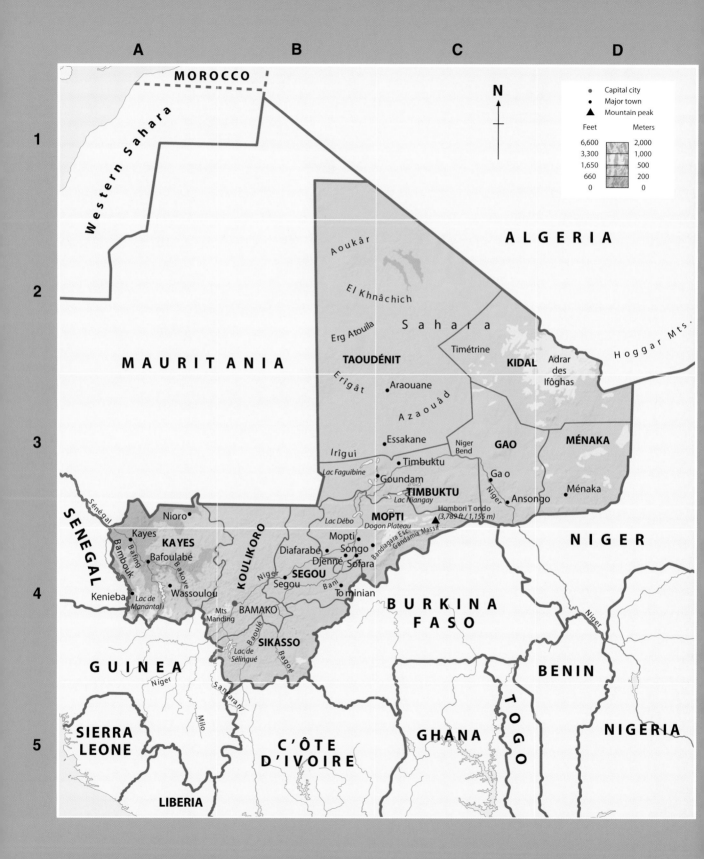

MAP OF MALI

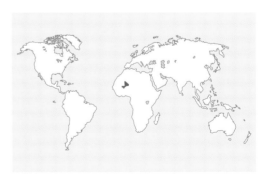

133

ECONOMIC MALI

Agriculture	Natural Resources	Services
Cattle	Salt Mines	Port
Cotton	Gold	 Airport
	Fish	

ABOUT THE ECONOMY

All figures are 2019 estimates unless otherwise noted.

OVERVIEW

Mali is a nation that depends on farming, yet much of its land is not suitable for agriculture. It ranks very low among the nations of the world in its economic development and in all economic statistics. Changes in climate put even greater pressure on farmers. More and more young people are leaving the country to look for work.

GROSS DOMESTIC PRODUCT (GDP)

$17.508 billion

WORKFORCE

agriculture 80 percent, services and industry 20 percent (2005)

AGRICULTURAL PRODUCTS

corn, rice, millet, sorghum, mangoes, cotton, watermelons, green onions, okra, sugar cane

INDUSTRIAL PRODUCTS

cotton, gold

CURRENCY

West African CFA franc (XOF)
$1 USD = 548.60 XOF

MAIN EXPORTS

cotton, gold, sesame seeds, lumber, vegetable oils

MAIN IMPORTS

petroleum, machinery and equipment, construction materials, medicines, textiles

TRADE PARTNERS

France, Senegal, China, Cote d'Ivoire, Switzerland, United Arab Emirates, Burkina Faso

INFLATION RATE

1.9 percent (2018)

PER CAPITA INCOME

$2,350

POPULATION BELOW POVERTY LINE

45 percent (2018)

EXTERNAL DEBT

$4.2 billion (2017)

ECONOMIC AID

$1.86 billion—from United States ($130 million), France, Canada, Netherlands, Germany, and others

MAJOR AIRPORTS

Bamako, Gao, Kayes, Mopti

PORTS

landlocked; river ports at Mopti and Bamako

CULTURAL MALI

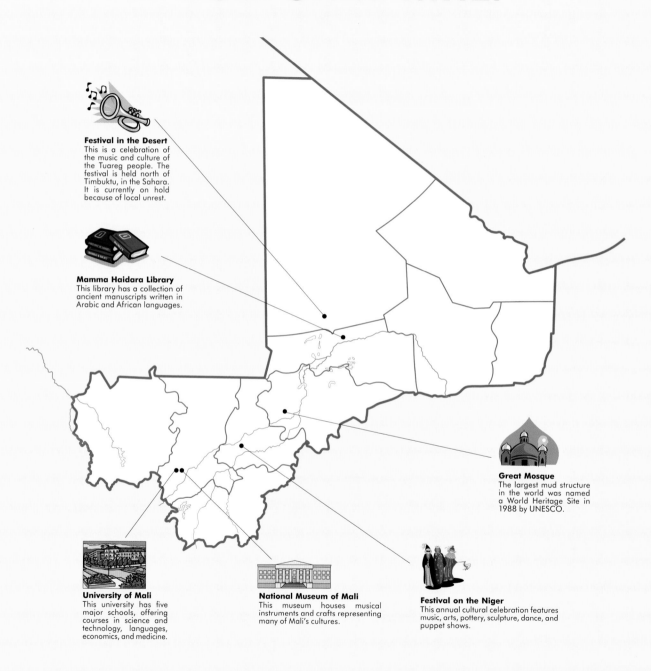

Festival in the Desert
This is a celebration of the music and culture of the Tuareg people. The festival is held north of Timbuktu, in the Sahara. It is currently on hold because of local unrest.

Mamma Haidara Library
This library has a collection of ancient manuscripts written in Arabic and African languages.

University of Mali
This university has five major schools, offering courses in science and technology, languages, economics, and medicine.

National Museum of Mali
This museum houses musical instruments and crafts representing many of Mali's cultures.

Great Mosque
The largest mud structure in the world was named a World Heritage Site in 1988 by UNESCO.

Festival on the Niger
This annual cultural celebration features music, arts, pottery, sculpture, dance, and puppet shows.

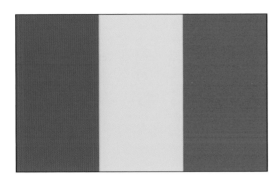

All figures are 2021 estimates unless otherwise noted.

OFFICIAL NAME
Republic of Mali

NATIONAL ANTHEM
"Le Mali," also known as "Pour l'Afrique et pour toi, Mali" ("For Africa and for you, Mali") or "A ton appel Mali" ("At your call, Mali").

CAPITAL
Bamako

ADMINISTRATIVE REGIONS
Gao, Kayes, Kidal, Koulikoro, Ménaka, Mopti, Ségou, Sikasso, Taoudenni (sometimes spelled Taoudénit), Timbuktu, District de Bamako

POPULATION
20.1 million

LIFE EXPECTANCY AT BIRTH
62 years

ETHNIC GROUPS
Bambara, Malinke, Fulani, Sarakole, Senufo, Songhai, Tuareg, Dogon, Bobo

LITERACY RATE
35.5 percent

LANGUAGES
French, Bambara

RELIGIONS
Islam 94 percent, animist 3 percent, Christian 3 percent

IMPORTANT ANNIVERSARY
Independence Day (September 22)

TIMELINE

IN MALI	IN THE WORLD
4th–8th century CE Mali is part of the Ghana empire.	**600 CE** The height of the Maya civilization is reached.
	1000 The Chinese perfect gunpowder and begin to use it in warfare.
1100 Timbuktu is founded by Turareg herdsmen.	
1235 Sundiata creates the Mali empire.	
1312 Mansa Musa becomes ruler.	
1324 Mansa Musa makes pilgrimage to Mecca.	
1337 Mansa Musa dies.	
1352 Ibn Battuta visits Mali.	
15th century Mali is ruled by the Songhai empire.	
16th century The Songhai empire collapses.	**1530** The beginning of the transatlantic slave trade is organized by the Portuguese in Africa.
	1558–1603 The reign of Elizabeth I of England takes place.
	1620 Pilgrims sail the *Mayflower* to America.
	1776 U.S. Declaration of Independence is written.
	1789–1799 The French Revolution occurs.
	1861 The American Civil War begins.
	1869 The Suez Canal is opened.
1892 Mali becomes a French colony.	**1914** World War I begins.
	1939 World War II begins.

IN MALI	IN THE WORLD
	1949 The North Atlantic Treaty Organization (NATO) is formed.
1960 Mali becomes independent.	
1960–1968 President Modibo Keita rules.	**1966–1969** The Chinese Cultural Revolution occurs.
1968 President Keita arrested by Lieutenant Moussa Traoré.	
1991 Moussa Traoré is arrested by Amadou Toumani Touré.	**1991** The Breakup of the Soviet Union occurs.
1992 Alpha Omar Konaré becomes president; he is reelected in 1997.	**1997** Hong Kong is returned to China.
	2001 Terrorists crash planes in New York, Washington, D.C., and Pennsylvania.
2002 Amadou Toumani Touré is elected president. Mali hosts Africa Cup of Nations.	**2003** The Iraq War begins.
2007 Tuareg rebels clash with armed forces.	**2008** Barack Obama is elected the United States' first African American president.
	2011 The United States officially declares an end to the Iraq War.
2012 A military coup removes Touré from office.	
2013 Ibrahim Boubacar Keïta is elected president; he is reelected in 2018.	
2015–2020 Islamic extremists increase activity and terrorize cities across the country.	**2016** Donald Trump is elected president of the United States.
	2018 Miguel Diaz-Canel is elected president of Cuba after nearly 60 years of the Castro family's rule.
2020 A military coup removes Keïta from office.	**2020–2021** The COVID-19 pandemic spreads around the world.

GLOSSARY

bògòlanfini
The Bambara word for mud cloth, a patterned cotton fabric dyed with mud.

Dogon
Cliff-dwelling people whose masked dances are widely known.

harmattan
A fierce wind that blows across the Sahara.

jinjinbere
A drink for special occasions made from water, sugar, lemon, and ginger.

mancala
A counting game played throughout Africa.

Sahel
The region of semidesert to the south of the Sahara; as the climate changes, more of this land turns to desert.

tagilmust
A headdress made of a long length of cloth that protects the wearer against the fierce harmattan and the sun.

Tuareg
A nomadic people who travel across the Sahara by camel.

FOR FURTHER INFORMATION

BOOKS

Niane, Djibril Tamsir. *Sundiata: An Epic of Old Mali*. Harlow, UK: Pearson Longman, 2006.

Schulz, Dorothea E. *Culture and Customs of Mali*. Santa Barbara, CA: Greenwood, 2012.

Wolny, Philip. *Discovering the Empire of Mali*. New York, NY: Rosen Central, 2014.

WEBSITES

Britannica Kids. Mali. kids.britannica.com/students/article/Mali/275638.

CIA. *The World Factbook*. "Mali." www.cia.gov/the-world-factbook/countries/mali.

Human Rights Watch. Mali. www.hrw.org/africa/mali.

FILMS

Bamako. New Yorker Films, 2006.

Behind the Blue Veil. Journeyman Pictures, 2013.

Mali Blues. Icarus Films, 2016.

BIBLIOGRAPHY

Cartwright, Mark. "Ghana Empire." World History Encyclopedia, March 5, 2019. www.ancient. eu/Ghana_Empire.

Cartwright, Mark. "Timbuktu." World History Encyclopedia, February 22, 2019. www.ancient. eu/Timbuktu.

CIA. *The World Factbook*. "Mali." www.cia.gov/the-world-factbook/countries/mali.

Clark, Andrew. "Mali." *Encyclopædia Britannica*, updated March 10, 2021. www.britannica.com/ place/Mali.

Coleman de Graft-Johnson, John. "Musa I of Mali." *Encyclopædia Britannica*, updated February 3, 2021. www.britannica.com/biography/Musa-I-of-Mali.

Diallo, Tiemoko, and Fadimata Kontao. "Mali President Claims Election Victory Amid Fraud Accusations." Reuters, August 14, 2018. www.reuters.com/article/us-mali-election/mali-president-claims-election-victory-amid-fraud-accusations-idUSKBN1KZ1GJ.

"France's Action in the Sahel." French Ministry for Europe and Foreign Affairs, updated April 2020. www.diplomatie.gouv.fr/en/french-foreign-policy/security-disarmament-and-non-proliferation/terrorism-france-s-international-action/article/france-s-action-in-the-sahel.

Konaté, Modibo. "Mali: Television." Media Landscapes. medialandscapes.org/country/mali/media/ television.

"Mali Announces New Government Following August Coup." Reuters, October 5, 2020. www. reuters.com/article/us-mali-security-government/mali-announces-new-government-following-august-coup-idUSKBN26Q2TP.

"Mali Empire." *Encyclopædia Britannica*, updated March 10, 2021. www.britannica.com/place/ Mali-historical-empire-Africa.

"Mali Exports, Imports, and Trade Partners." Observatory of Economic Complexity. oec.world/ en/profile/country/mli.

"Mali: Government." Michigan State University. globaledge.msu.edu/countries/mali/government.

"Mali Profile — Timeline." BBC News, August 26, 2020. www.bbc.com/news/world-africa-13881978.

"The Military Intervention in Mali and Beyond: An Interview with Bruno Charbonneau." Oxford Research Group, March 28, 2019. www.oxfordresearchgroup.org.uk/blog/the-french-intervention-in-mali-an-interview-with-bruno-charbonneau.

"Republic of Mali." ElectionGuide. www.electionguide.org/countries/id/133.

"Sundiata Keita." *Encyclopædia Britannica*, updated January 1, 2021. www.britannica.com/ biography/Sundiata-Keita.

"Water, Sanitation and Hygiene." UNICEF Mali. www.unicef.org/mali/en/water-sanitation-and-hygiene.

INDEX

INDEX